THE FIRE
of
LITTLE JIM

THE FIRE
of
LITTLE JIM

Power for Growth from the Letter of James

William E. Hulme

"Today or tomorrow I will set a bright fire
with little Jim."
—Martin Luther, *Table Talk*

ABINGDON
Nashville

THE FIRE OF LITTLE JIM

Copyright © 1976 by Abingdon

Library of Congress Cataloging in Publication Data

Hulme, William Edward, 1920-
   The fire of little Jim.
   1. Bible. N.T. James—Criticism, interpretation, etc. I.
Title.
BS 2785.2.H84   227'.91'06   76-13535

ISBN 0-687-13090-5

MANUFACTURED BY THE PARTHENON PRESS AT
NASHVILLE, TENNESSEE, UNITED STATES OF AMERICA

To my family,
each of whom has contributed
to this book

Contents

Introduction

The New Testament Letter of James "spoke" to me in a time of crisis, when our family experienced a sudden and devastating tragedy in the death of our oldest daughter. I am not sure why I turned to this letter in my need, for I had read it and studied it many times before and had no distinct recollection of its value. There is an aimlessness of behavior in crisis times that matches the loss of moorings and goals in one's perspective. Having once turned to James, however, I began to receive what evidently I needed, since I purposefully returned to the letter again and again.

Clarity and Confidence

In retrospect, I suppose what caught the attention of my scattered mind in that first reading was the clarity of the letter in areas which are often murky in our general thought and poignantly so in times of crisis. This clarity is specifically evident in the following areas:

1. In contrast to the superficiality with which it is usually delineated, in the Letter of James the sphere of

the "world"—the well-known biblical symbol for the social locality of evil—is depicted in a way that penetrates life-styles supposedly safe from its influence. James sees the "world" in specific values and priorities rather than in specific behaviors.

2. In sharp contrast to his description of the world, James delineates the values and priorities of life as it is shaped by the "faith of our Lord Jesus Christ." His differentiation between these two spheres of influence centers in the desires and attitudes of the human spirit.

3. James unequivocally affirms the freedom and power of the individual person. In times of crisis one is more aware of one's impotency than of one's power. One's freedom becomes an abstraction which is deluged by negative feelings. James throws out the lifeline.

The needs that I experienced in my time of crisis were obviously particular and temporary, at least in their intensity. Yet I am convinced that they are also general and continuous. Subsequent to my experience with James, I have attempted to utilize the themes of his letter as resources in pastoral counseling. Knowing full well the particularity of my own appreciation, I was prepared for a lack of response from the counselees. Instead I was impressed by the opposite. There was probably a contagion factor—my obvious appreciation being perceived by the counselee—but the way in which these persons responded has convinced me that James speaks to universal human needs.

In the past decade many movements emphasizing ways and means of effecting change in human living have emerged with phenomenal popular response. People obviously long for change and want very much to believe they have the freedom and power to effect it. So we have had—and still have—the workshops in Transactional Analysis (T.A.), the schools of Transcendental Meditation (T.M.), the classes in Parent Effectiveness Training (P.E.T.), and the courses in the Silva Method of Mind Control, to name some of the more prominent of these movements. In contrast to these, James does not present the *techniques* for effective change. Rather, he affirms the power for change that is ours through the faith of our Lord Jesus Christ.

This affirmation contrasts with a lot of fuzziness on this point in Christian circles, where the prevailing impression is often of human impotency and bondage rather than of power and freedom. During a discussion in a Silva Mind Control class on the negative potential of fear, self-doubt, and guilt, a young woman made the observation that the Judeo-Christian heritage seems to have impressed these negative emotions upon our culture. Engaging in conversation with her later, I commented that, while many shared her observation, and undoubtedly with good reason, the irony is that the Christian message is the Good News of reconciliation that puts an end to these negativities. She evidenced genuine surprise. "That's not what it's been in my life," she said.

The Christian tradition's focus on the "poor miserable sinner" is so prolonged in practice that it rarely shifts to "the power to become the sons of God" (familiar phrases in Christian worship services that indicate a spiritual progression). We have been programmed for defeat rather than for victory.

In his clear perception of the differences between the spirit of the world and the Spirit of God, James focuses on another need which has received much attention from contemporary self-improvement groups, namely, the need for identity. The prevailing confusion over these differences undermines the basis for establishing not only who we are but *whose* we are. People who consider themselves "good citizens" are susceptible to being brainwashed by circumstances into becoming involved in unethical if not criminal activities. We see this tendency in the frequently uncovered betrayals of trust among persons in high places. It occurs also among lesser personages in a myraid of ways, only some of which become publicly exposed. When we are hazy concerning our identity, our hierarchy of values rests on "shifting sand." For James this identity, or self-image, is established by a clear-cut perception of loyalty and of belonging.

Changing and Coping

This past year I have served as a part-time chaplain in a general hospital. On one occasion I asked an apparently receptive patient, who was facing serious surgery the following morning, whether he would like me to pray with him. He looked somewhat discomfited and said something to the effect that he knew very little about prayer. "In fact," he said, "I only know one prayer." Suspecting this to be the Lord's Prayer, I nevertheless asked which it was. With little hesitation he said, "Lord, grant me the courage to change the things that can be changed, to accept the things that cannot be changed, and the wisdom to know the difference." I had an idea why he knew this prayer. "Alcoholics Anonymous?" I asked. "Right," he said. I used the structure of this prayer in praying with him about his surgery.

Although the prayer adopted by Alcoholics Anonymous is of relatively recent origin in its wording, its substance contains the gist of the Letter of James. James' affirmation of human freedom and power is an appeal to his readers to utilize these resources to change what can and should be changed. At the same time he gives full cognizance to the formidable obstacles that hinder the fulfillment of some of our needs. The prime example is the powerlessness of the poor to change the exploitive practices of the rich. The poor may be able to do no more than endure this exploitation. For James, endurance is the equivalent of accepting what cannot be changed.

Gaining the wisdom to know the difference between what can and cannot be changed is just as important as possessing the courage to change or to endure. James not only delineates the nature of this wisdom, which he calls the "wisdom from above," but reaffirms the Old Testament theme that such wisdom is available from God to those who ask with singleness of mind.

We are frequently reminded that we cannot change the world! History is tragically filled with the wreckage of utopian dreams and programs as well as with the disillusioned dreamers. We cannot always change even our own immediate environment. In spite of the limitations on changing the world, James affirms that we can change *ourselves*. In so far as we change, we actually effect a change in our environment. We can influence others, and subsequently, in however minute a degree, we do effect a change in the world.

But James is not one of those proponents of self-improvement who believe that the way to change society is to change individuals. He attacks the problems of society directly. He not only speaks for the poor, he speaks to the poor. Whatever focus he places on the individual is always within the context of the social order and its problems. When revolution is in the air as it has been in recent times, people who are chafing against societal exploitation are rarely sympathetic to movements that focus on the development of their *adaptive* potentials. Karl Marx called such an approach, unfortunately identified as religion, "the opium of the people," and the poor blacks, Indians, Chicanos, and whites of this country apparently feel the same way.

James not only acknowledges the problems of society, he also examines them. Evil is a reality in the world which he denounces in no uncertain terms. Yet he believes it can be endured. Evil is no illusion: the only illusion is the spurious hierarchy of values spawned by evil. James describes and then denounces the social exploitation of the poor by the privileged and powerful. Though his counsel to the poor is to cope with their sufferings on the basis of hope, such hope is always in the context of self-affirmation and action. As a social critic James possesses the rare balance of being concerned about the personal and even intra-psychic dimensions of human life as well as about the corporate dimensions of our social existence. The help that he offers is given in full acknowledgment of the tragically evil consequences of social injustice.

James speaks to universal human need because he offers help where people tend to feel helpless. He is positive where too often the religious tradition has been negative. He is down-to-earth and concrete in contrast to the frequent abstractions of theologians. He offers practical help for personal living.

The Structure of the Letter

As a Catholic Epistle, the letter is addressed to all Christians. James directs it to "the twelve tribes in the Dispersion," a symbolic term for the New Testament Israel dispersed in the world. The letter had difficulty becoming incorporated into the New Testament canon and, even after its incorporation, has had difficulty in gaining appreciation. Different in style and content from other biblical epistles, it has no explicit references to Jesus' death and resurrection and mentions his name only twice.

Little is known of its origin. Although some of the early church fathers attributed it to the James who was the brother of Jesus, this is now largely discounted. Written in excellent Greek, the letter first appeared in the Greek section of the church, in which it also had its earliest support.

The style is similar to the diatribe format of ancient Greek literature, a type of moral address in which the subject matter was introduced by an imaginary questioner asking brief questions and giving equally brief answers. Imperative in style, the diatribe depended on its broad directing motivation for its unity rather than on any logical structure. These are also the characteristics of the Letter of James.

James emphasizes several Old Testament themes and

uses Old Testament personalities as his models. The acquisition of wisdom and the call to repentance for social injustices are two such themes that permeate the letter, and Job, Elijah, and the prophets in general are singled out as illustrations of James' points. This has led some to question whether the letter was not originally a tract of Jewish rather than Christian origin.

Though James is obviously a Jew, his letter just as obviously belongs to the New Testament. Its basic theme of the law of liberty is described in deliberate contrast to the Old Testament law. The phrase "the faith of our Lord Jesus Christ," though used only once, is implicitly integral to the total context. There are repeated correspondences to the Sermon on the Mount, especially the Beatitudes. Some scholars have also observed a resemblance to I Peter. James' polemical treatment of justification by faith reflects an explicitly New Testament theme of the early centuries of Christendom, and his peculiar treatment of it became a controversial issue during the Reformation. The letter was not simply edited by a Christian, but was written in its entirety by a Christian.

Thematic Integration

This book is not a commentary on the Letter of James. Rather it is a development of the basic themes of the letter as these relate to human need and to the ways in which we live together in human society. As has been noted, the letter is not integrated in a structural sense. On the contrary, it may give the impression that its author was directed more by impulse than by logical train of thought. There is little logical sequence or transition between the various subjects that he treats. On the other hand, a more careful reading reveals a thematic integration. The author holds forth certain basic themes which he weaves in and out of his letter. These themes are very significant for human living in our day as well as in that of James, and it is these themes that form the basis for this book. They are its table of contents.

The order in which I present and develop these themes is similar to that of the letter. However, I have adjusted this order in specific instances to enhance the sense of movement and direction. Prior to each theme and its development I have collected the sections of the letter that pertain to it.

The first chapter of the letter sets the stage for what follows. Each of the themes save one has a reference in this chapter. In utilizing James' themes as my format, therefore, I am in this sense building on the same structural foundation. My style, however, is not that of the diatribe, for the book is an exposition of the themes as they relate to human living and human need.

There are a few repetitions in the sections of the letter that precede each chapter. This is an overlap reflecting the overlap one would naturally anticipate in this number of themes. Yet the fact that there are so few repetitions is an indication of the distinctiveness of each of these areas.

The value of the Letter of James has been hidden behind its surface shortcomings and its differences from other Christian writings. Consequently the letter has not received the attention or appreciation that it deserves.

From the early centuries of the Christian era through the Middle Ages and the Reformation to the present time, it has occupied only a peripheral position in biblical interest. This has been a loss. It is hoped that the loss will not be perpetuated.

I

The Evil Division of Rich and Poor

Let the lowly brother boast in his exaltation, and the rich in his humiliation, because like the flower of the grass he will pass away. For the sun rises with its scorching heat and withers the grass; its flower falls, and its beauty perishes. So will the rich man fade away in the midst of his pursuits. (James 1:9-11)

You have dishonored the poor man. Is it not the rich who oppress you, is it not they who drag you into court? Is it not they who blaspheme the honorable name which was invoked over you? (James 2:6-7)

Come now, you rich, weep and howl for the miseries that are coming upon you. Your riches have rotted and your garments are moth-eaten. Your gold and silver have rusted, and their rust will be evidence against you and will eat your flesh like fire. You have laid up treasure for the last days. Behold, the wages of the laborers who mowed your fields, which you kept back by fraud, cry out; and the cries of the harvesters have reached the ears of the Lord of hosts. You have lived on the earth in luxury and in pleasure; you have fattened your hearts in a day of slaughter. You have condemned, you have killed the righteous man; he does not resist you. (James 5:1-6)

James is a New Testament version of an Old Testament prophet. In the book of Acts and in the Epistles of Paul, references are made to the gift of prophecy in the church. The New Testament prophet was one who received a message or oracle for the people from God and spoke it. James was not a prophet in this sense. The Old Testament prophet also proclaimed to the people the oracles of God which he received by revelation. These messages were quite diverse in content. The well-known prophets, however, spoke specifically as social critics. They were God's spokespersons regarding the ways in which people were relating to each other in their life in community. It is in this sense that James is a prophet.

The Prophet's Function

Like his Old Testament counterpart, James identifies with the sufferings of those who are exploited by the social structures. He empathizes in a very partisan way with the poor. He suffers with them in their afflictions. These afflictions stir up within him a reflection of the wrath of God. The poor—the have-nots—are the victims of social injustices which outrage the compassionate sensibilities of the prophet.

Lincoln is credited with saying that God must have loved the poor because he made so many of them. The fallacy in this observation of the poor lies not in their numbers but in the assumption that their poorness is God's doing. The poor are created by human society in violation of God's design. The very word *poor* is a symbol of the accumulated evils of a man-made segregation—a denial of the basic equality of all human beings in the uniqueness of their persons.

To James this division into rich and poor is evil: "Come now, you rich, weep and howl for the miseries that are coming upon you. . . . Behold, the wages of the laborers who mowed your fields, which you kept back by fraud, cry out." In this denunciation he echoes the Old Testament prophets. Jeremiah warned:

> Woe to him who builds his house by unrighteousness,
>   and his upper rooms by injustice;
> who makes his neighbor serve him for nothing,
>   and does not give him his wages. (Jer. 22:13)

Isaiah denounces the same evil practice:

> Woe to those who join house to house,
>   who add field to field,
> until there is no more room. (Isa. 5:8)

The prophet of doom, Amos, makes a similar charge:

> Hear this, you who trample upon the needy,
>   and bring the poor of the land to an end,
> saying, "When will the new moon be over,
>   that we may sell grain?
> And the sabbath,
>   that we may offer wheat for sale,
> that we may make the ephah small and
>   the shekel great,
>   and deal deceitfully with false balances,
> that we may buy the poor for silver
>   and the needy for a pair of sandals,
>   and sell the refuse of the wheat?" (Amos 8:4-6)

The merchant class chided by Amos is also a target for James: "Come now, you who say, 'Today or tomorrow we will go into such and such a town and spend a year there and trade and get gain'" (4:13).

James issues the call to repentance in a way familiar to the prophets: "Cleanse your hands, you sinners, and purify your hearts, you men of double mind. Be wretched and mourn and weep" (4:8-9). These words are reminiscent of the prophet Jeremiah, who exhorted Jerusalem, "Wash your heart from wickedness" (Jer. 4:14). Also Isaiah: "Wash you, make you clean; put away the evil of your doings from before mine eyes" (Isa. 1:16 King James Version).

The concentration rather than the distribution of wealth is based upon and leads to social structures that oppress some to the advantage of others. In fact, the attraction of money lies not only in its exchange value for material possessions but also in its potential for power. James, like his Old Testament counterparts, holds the rich—the haves—responsible for this oppression: they have the power! They can change the things that need to be changed; but they lack the motivation—the *courage.* The poor have no such power. Their only recourse for change is violent revolution. James does not acknowledge this possibility. Rather he focuses on the haves, who hold the key to change in society and do not use it.

Hope for Redemption

Like the Old Testament prophets James does more than denounce the evil. He holds out the hope of God's redeeming action. The difference in status between the haves and the have-nots is an illusion to begin with. The imbalance can be reversed by societal changes in evaluation. "How are the mighty fallen!" is a familiar commentary on the historical process. James and the prophets see this reversal as God's redemptive action on behalf of the oppressed. God will make low the rich and exalt the poor. In fact, because the difference in status is in itself an illusion, God's reversal of these values is already in effect. Therefore, "let the lowly brother boast in his exaltation, and the rich in his humiliation." This elevation of the poor parallels the beatitude "Blessed are the poor" (Luke 6:20 KJV).

The effects of the illusory difference in status, however, are not illusory: oppression is real. The poor cry out because of it, and God hears the cry; yet the exploitation and affliction may continue. How long, O Lord, how long will you delay? James' response is a call to patience. The Lord will come. In the meantime the wait is like that of a farmer for the rains that will mature his crop. Waiting for the rain is not an easy wait; yet we wait. So also wait in your afflictions. God will not abandon the afflicted. His compassion is too essential to his nature for him to do so. God's faithfulness is the basis of the believer's hope and the motivation for the prophet's encouraging words to trust. The Creator is not under the same illusions as his fallen creation, and he will redeem the victims of the tragic consequences of these illusions.

Opening the Channels of Communication

In the meantime the prophet devotes his energies to reconciliation. The interim is a time for healing in our relationships. The call to repentance is for the purpose of clearing the channels of communication with God and with our neighbors. It is not just the rich who sin. All are sinners. James takes this prophetic insight to its limits. If anyone keeps the whole law of God but fails in just one point, he is guilty on all points.

It may, however, be more difficult for the rich to repent. Repentance means experiencing a change of heart. Since the rich hold the key to social change, a change of heart on their part would move them to seek an end to this unfortunate division of humanity. But it is a sober historical observation that the haves do not as a rule initiate or voluntarily give up their disproportionate power. They appear more often to instigate social welfare—giving gifts to the poor—rather than social changes in the distribution of power and privilege.

Repentance begins with confession. As we confess to God—and to each other—we clear away the obstacle to communication. The potential intimacy of the human community depends upon the humility of openness. For James this openness, this humility, is made possible by "the law of liberty," "the faith of our Lord Jesus Christ," the Good News of the merciful love of God. It is God's reconciling nature—as revealed in the faith of our Lord Jesus Christ—that not only makes repentance a natural process in human development but also makes it a means for reconciliation in the human community.

Distortions in Cultural Evaluation

Though James' prophetic function influences each of his themes, we are concentrating in this chapter on the specific theme of the categories of rich and poor, which are based on distortions in the evaluative processes of human society. Perhaps the majority of us do not identify ourselves with either of these categories. In the United States of America the rich and the poor are minorities, with the larger middle class constituting the majority. This is not the case in many of the so-called underdeveloped countries. If we use again the terms *haves* and *have-nots* we may find a readier identification, particularly if we view these categories on a global scale.

From a global perspective just to be an American is to be a have. To illustrate the point with statistics from the Interreligious Foundation for Community Organization, if the world were a global village of one hundred people, seventy of them would be unable to read, and only one would have a college education. Over fifty would be suffering from malnutrition, and over eighty would live in what we call substandard housing. Only six of these hundred would be Americans. These six would have half the village's entire income, and the other ninety-four would exist on the other half. Righting the disproportion of this global division would mean a lowering of our standard of living, since there are not enough resources to enable the rest of the world to live as do Americans. Our leadership evidently believes that this kind of sacrifice is more than most Americans are willing to make.

Not all Americans are haves, even by global standards. In the midst of our affluent society there is grinding poverty, of which the migrant farm worker is an example. He is paid around $1,500 a year. If everyone in the family worked, the family might make $2,700. His life expectancy is only forty-nine years. Babies as well as the mothers giving birth to them have twice the average American mortality rate. If a family have two rooms in which to live they can be considered fortunate. None of the family would be likely to reach the eighth grade.

The system of values that sustains these categories of rich and poor is so deeply ingrained in our culture that even people who are sensitive to the Christian gospel are influenced by it. The hierarchy of importances and priorities that exalt the rich and humble the poor have an entrenched credibility despite their illusory character. Yet in the midst of their pursuits, the rich will pass away. Their tenure as exalted people is short—like the life of a flower. The rose that is in full bloom today may begin to wither by tomorrow. The tangible possessions that constitute being rich have a built-in destructibility that ensures their transiency. What does not succumb to "rot" and decay may "rust away" or be "eaten by moths."

This reference by James to nature's agents of destruction is reminiscent of Jesus' admonition in the Sermon on the Mount not to lay up treasures on earth, where moth and rust consume. Rot, rust, and moth challenge the illusion of durability that surrounds material possessions.

The realist who sees through the illusion lays up treasures in heaven, where neither moth nor rust consumes. He looks with eyes not fully conditioned by cultural values and sees the reversal of status hidden behind these values. The first shall be last, and the last shall be first.

The Blessedness and Curse of Poverty

The Christian tradition's emphasis on the implicit reversal in status of the rich and the poor has inspired some notable endeavors in the adoption of poverty, of which the most well-known is that of Francis of Assisi. In our own country Henry David Thoreau lived by choice on the bare essentials in his Walden experiment and praised the poor in his journal. "Give me the poverty that enjoys true wealth," he wrote. "Farmers are respectable and interesting to me in proportion as they are poor—poor farmers."

Francis and Thoreau are imitated today by those—often in the counterculture—who have adopted a life of simplicity in protest of our affluent life-styles. Though this movement seems to be on the wane, poverty is still an "in" thing with some of the children of affluent Americans, who are seeking at least a partial immunity from the corrupting influence of the distorted priorities inherent in affluence.

But Francis, Thoreau, and their counterculture imitators missed the debilitating side effects of poverty. The voluntary poor established their self-image in the affluent society prior to becoming poor. Francis was reared in wealth; Thoreau was a Harvard graduate; most of the counterculture poor are middle-class, college-educated dropouts. Poverty does not crush their egos as it does those of people who were reared in it. The prophets perceived and protested this cruel blow to personal worth and dignity which poverty inflicts. When poverty is not a matter of choice, its effect on the human spirit is quite different from when it is. The image of deprivation may remain fixed in the psyche after one's poverty is eased. Even the subsequent possession of great wealth may not erase the early scar of insecurity. Some who endured the Great Depression, for example, were so traumatized by the experience that they were irrationally preoccupied with money long after they had attained what others would have considered financial security. The contrast between the personal security over material possessions of those reared in wealth and the insecurity associated with the *nouveau riche* is another frequent indication that the stigma of poverty leaves its mark on one's self-image.

Concentration Depends upon Exploitation

The concentration of wealth in the hands of some of the people depends upon the exploitation of the rest. Those who suffer this exploitation most acutely are the poor. The charge which James levels against the rich is that they have made their pile at the expense of other people. The miserable wages they pay to those who mow their fields is to him tantamount to fraud.

It is easier to point the finger at the employer than at those of us who encourage him. We are all attracted to bargains, which in itself seems a relatively harmless passion. However, our bargains may be at someone else's expense. That someone else is often the defrauded laborer—the migrant worker, the nonunionized worker, someone not covered by the minimum wage law, the native worker in an American industry overseas.

But James has a greater indictment than that of fraud. The rich have "fattened [their] hearts in a day of slaughter." Regardless of what James may have had in mind by this accusation, it is an apt description of the war profiteer. Commenting upon the fact that both sides in the 1974 war in Cyprus were being supplied with

American arms, a news analyst quipped that this was bad news for the Greek and Turkish Cypriots but good news for the American munitions makers.

So it is that the advantages of wealth, status, and power for one group are to the disadvantage of another; the comfort of affluence enjoyed by one class creates discomfort for another class. Our problem as indirect exploiters is that we are reluctant to see the full consequences of our advantages, preferring instead a superimposed ignorance to protect us from whatever sensitivities remain with our consciences. But the prophet in our midst makes it difficult for us to remain ignorant. Is it any wonder, then, that he has often suffered for his message—all the way from taunts and ostracism to jail and martyrdom? The first martyr of the Christian church, Stephen, laid it on the line when he challenged his countrymen by asking, "Which of the prophets did not your fathers persecute?" (Acts 7:52). Since we have been on the advantaged side of the disproportion for so long, we have assumed this as our right. Such is not the case, however, and those who do not of their own volition seek to distribute the treasures of the earth more equitably may be forced to do so. As the power and wealth of the so-called Third World increases, the power and wealth of the so-called developed countries may become commensurably less.

Money as a Symbol

The symbol of wealth, of course, is money. Money is obviously a medium of exchange and not an end in itself. Yet in collecting the stuff we have made it an end in itself. Its strange symbolic value is traced by psychoanalysts to the infant's fascination with and hoarding of his own feces. This connotation is implicit in the King James Version's use of the term "filthy lucre" for money. In the peculiar attraction which money holds for us, as well as in our uneasiness over this attraction, we are, in Freudian terms, fixated at the anal stage of our development.

Money is a promissory note, ostensibly for silver or gold. It also promises much more—status and power and personal worth. Our culture generally accepts the acquisition of money as a valid motivation for participation in any lawful activity, as well as a sometimes accepted rationalization for some illegal corner-cutting. This acquisition may have little to do with providing daily bread. Professional athletes making hundreds of thousands of dollars a year may hold out for more at contract time. The so-called captains of industry collect astronomical salaries as a symbol of their position, and some labor leaders are not far behind. Affluent people are often more bargain-conscious than the poor: the economical supermarkets and discount stores are usually located in the suburbs. "I need the money" and "I'm doing it for the money" are accepted as justifiable reasons for all kinds of activities.

The moths and the rust exist as a judgment upon our fixation about collecting money. Whether it is collected for its own sake, or used as a means of collecting *things*, our passion for money has its built-in corrosive. Neither money, nor the things it can buy, nor the power and prestige they bring, have any lasting value in themselves.

Striving after money because of what supposedly it can

do for us is destructive to human fulfillment because it is a distortion of human values. It carries with it its own judgment. We can see this most clearly in the wrecked political careers of capable people who, though affluent on any comparative basis, were driven, by whatever demons of destruction, to strive for more. Their talents were frustrated and their service ended when they succumbed to the temptation to use their position as a means for collecting additional money.

The disease is widespread and no respecter of persons. Some, of course, do not get caught by the law. Yet even those who are scrupulously honest may still suffer the erosion of their own potential as persons because of their addiction to money. If the love of it is not *the* root of all evil, it is at least *a* root of all evil.

Those who are deprived of money are deprived of power and self-esteem as well as of sustenance. The exploitation that makes possible the concentration of wealth also creates the poor. David Kunst, who walked around the world, was impressed by a kind of poverty that he felt did not exist in developed countries like his own United States of America. But though our poor are not poor by the standards of Calcutta, they may suffer a similar kind of personal deprivation. To be at the bottom economically in one's society is to be powerless in that society. The frustration is due not simply to hunger but to the abuse inflicted on one's self-image. Giving someone food stamps does not satisfy his need for self-esteem.

Other Kinds of Poverty

The psychologist Abraham Maslow believes that human beings are motivated to satisfy certain basic needs. These needs follow a definite progressive order in which one need must be satisfied before a person is motivated to focus on the next need. At the rudimentary level are the basic physiological needs. Next are the safety needs. These are followed by the need for love and belonging. After this is the need for self-esteem. Finally there is the need for self-actualization. If people are hungry their need for safety and love and self-esteem and self-actualization is considerably lessened by the disproportionate need for food. On the other hand, if someone is reasonably safe and his belly is full, he becomes concerned about belonging and being loved. Finally, if his basic need for belonging and for self-esteem is met, he is in a position to be concerned about the development of his potential as a self.

According to this delineation of basic needs, a person can be poverty-stricken because of the lack of satisfaction of any one or several of them. His awareness of each particular poverty is dependent upon the satisfaction of the preceding need on the progressive scale. But if a need has been met previously so that he feels secure in it, he can tolerate a temporary deprivation of satisfaction of that need and still pursue the satisfaction of needs further along the progressive scale.

If Maslow is correct, people are not going to be much interested in the freedom for self-actualization, for example, if they are chronically hungry. As one citizen of an underdeveloped country experiencing the novelty of democracy put it, "Sure we have a lot more freedoms, but it's all I can do to feed my family, much less send my children to school." It is not uncommon for people to exchange their freedom for sufficient food and safety when these more rudimentary needs are not being met.

One of the basic goals of Communism is to meet the rudimentary needs of the masses for food, clothing, and shelter. Consequently the Communist approach is attractive when people are hungry. But the system lacks an awareness of the complexity of human nature. Concerned with the economic dimensions of human life, the Communist ideal of the equalization or commonality of material possessions fails to reckon with the discontent that may subsequently emerge when people are free to focus on needs further up the scale. The Communist model has no built-in adaptation to dissent and hence has consistently relied on threatening people's need for safety in order to maintain the system. The result is another kind of poverty. Those whose safety is threatened are deprived of power by those who possess it, and this unequalization or lack of commonality of power has a way of unequalizing once again the possession of material things. The concentration of power is as corrupting to those who hold it as the deprivation of power is impoverishing to those who lack it.

Winners and Losers

The global dimensions of exploitation are mirrored in our social structures. The free enterprise system fosters a spirit of competition in which the syndrome of winners and losers, drawn from athletics, prevails. The poor are obviously losers. In fact, they do not even enter the competition. This in itself contributes to a sense of worthlessness. Competition has its defenders, who insist that it brings out the best in each "contestant," and in the business world prevents exploitation of the consumer public. What we fail to realize is that we have come to depend on it for these values, and therefore justify it rather than seek to achieve these values in some other way.

The competitive labels "winners" and "losers" are an illusion: winners are also in a sense losers. This is because the value system that supports the ego boost we receive from winning is itself illusory. Self-esteem is basically derived from love and not from power. Although one whose self-esteem is based on love also has power, the reverse is not true: power in itself does not produce love. As a basis for self-esteem the possession of power depends on being a successful competitor, whereas love depends on a spirit of cooperation and trust. The reality that is hidden by the illusory values of a competitive system is that everybody benefits from cooperation. This is the true wisdom. All are winners. A person does not have to defeat or be defeated; he can negotiate with the other so that each can win—as the great arbitrators know. Cooperation and competition rarely go together; one tends to cancel out the other.

A society that is built on the illusory values of a competitive system is designed to favor the exploiter. The status-seekers can play a ruthless game. They are not "hindered" by the restraints of a social conscience or by sensitivity to the needs of others. In fact, our very participation in the competitive world diminishes these sensitivities and compassions. Moral questions are easily rationalized, if not cynically dismissed. It is a battle milieu which, as we say, "divides the men from the boys." The very terms in this cliché not only reflect a male chauvinism and a distorted concept of masculinity but also indicate which sex is most responsible for dividing the world into winners and losers. In terms of the values based on cooperation, the comparison in the cliché is reversed. Although the "boys" are "zeroed" by the competition, they are "closer to the angels." As James says, they may not even resist their oppressors. Or as Thoreau put it, "If a man does not keep pace with his companions, perhaps it is because he hears a different drummer." He may perceive the hidden reality, the true wisdom. So if he suffers, he suffers in hope.

II

In Suffering—Endure

Count it all joy, my brethren, when you meet various trials, for you know that the testing of your faith produces steadfastness. And let steadfastness have its full effect, that you may be perfect and complete, lacking in nothing. (James 1:2-4)

Blessed is the man who endures trial, for when he has stood the test he will receive the crown of life which God has promised to those who love him. (James 1:12)

Be patient, therefore, brethren, until the coming of the Lord. Behold, the farmer waits for the precious fruit of the earth, being patient over it until it receives the early and the late rain. You also be patient. Establish your hearts, for the coming of the Lord is at hand. Do not grumble, brethren, against one another, that you may not be judged; behold, the Judge is standing at the doors. As an example of suffering and patience, brethren, take the prophets who spoke in the name of the Lord. Behold, we call those happy who were steadfast. You have heard of the steadfastness of Job, and you have seen the purpose of the Lord, how the Lord is compassionate and merciful. (James 5:7-11)

The Gamut of Suffering

There are other sufferings in this world than those caused by the deprivations of poverty. The advantaged also suffer. Suffering is no respecter of persons, class, or creed. It is "man," and not a particular kind of man, that is "chastened with pain upon his bed, / and with continual strife in his bones" (Job 33:19). The rich, like the poor, are afflicted with physical and mental illness. They too may lose their sense of meaning and worth and suffer the pains of loneliness, family strife, and estrangement. Rich and poor alike are afflicted with anxiety over loved ones, grief over departed ones, and the dread of their own approaching death. Suffering is associated with death. Like death it is a lonely experience. Its pains may be severe enough even to move the sufferer to wish for death. In death the differentiation between rich and poor is meaningless and the illusion of class and status is gone. As the suffering Job put it, "Naked came I from my mother's womb, and naked shall I return."

Despite the universality of suffering and its seeming inherence in human life, sufferings of all kinds are exacerbated by our distorted priorities. Though progress has been made in medical care, for example, such care is still of low priority in our national budgets. The amount of money spent on defense far exceeds that devoted to medical research, schools, hospitals, and other health care programs. Violent deaths cut a wide swath of suffering. Wars and highway accidents account for the majority of these. We could greatly reduce the number of violent deaths if we were determined to do so. Speed and liquor, for example, are involved in most of the traffic fatalities. Both can be curtailed. The energy crisis has already reduced our speed. What can move us to reduce the drinking problem?

Technology is a mixed blessing even in peacetime.

With the help of machines we get more done, but our bodies are less involved. The result is that diet and exercise programs have become big business. The by-products of industry have poisoned our environment. The air we breathe, the water we drink, and the food we eat are all adversely affected by this darker side of technology. None of these pollutions is a problem in Vilcabamba, Ecuador, in Hunza, Kashmir, or in the Caucasus Mountains in southwestern Russia, where a significantly higher percentage of people live beyond a century in reasonably good health.

Churches may also become distorted in their priorities. The ministry of reconciliation and spiritual development has at times been superseded by the more tangible success symbols associated with institutional expansion. The concern for property and progress has corrupted churches as it has other human institutions. The result has been institutional development at the expense of spiritual sensitivity and personal wholeness.

The fact that each of us tends at times to be self-centered and insensitive takes its inevitable toll of suffering. Our turned-inward-ness not only isolates us emotionally from others but is in itself destructive; it can inflict pain upon others and sabotage our own peace and self-esteem. These negative tendencies are verbalized in our quips and proverbs. "He is his own worst enemy," we say, or, "People are like porcupines if you get too close."

The prophet who has protested against the social injustices that have brought suffering to the poor has himself repeatedly suffered because of his protest. When Jesus said that a prophet was not without honor save in his home country, he was referring to himself. His

warning proved correct when he was forcibly ejected
from his hometown of Nazareth and subsequently put to
death by the leaders of his nation because he threatened
the social order. As a prophet he had denounced this
leadership for its exploitation of the masses. His cross
has become the symbol of suffering by dissenters and
protesters at the hands of the established order.

The fact that all life ends in death, despite social
reforms, scientific advances, and personal wholeness,
means that sickness and loss are endemic to human life.
A newspaper columnist who lost his son in a mountain
climbing accident wrote in a subsequent column that,
since such tragedies are a part of life, he was aware that
in having five children he was raising his chances of
experiencing them.

James' Old Testament model, Job, is known both for
his suffering and for his protest against suffering. He
anguished over the seeming meaninglessness of his
sufferings and challenged God to show any just cause for
them. Like Elihu, Job's fourth counselor, James empathizes with the sufferer's search for meaning. I had
used the book of Job many times in teaching pastoral
counseling, and felt I could understand how Job felt, but
in retrospect I believe that I identified more with Elihu
than with Job. In suffering the tragic death of our
daughter my identification was obviously with Job. In
this state of mind I turned to the Letter of James and
found it speaking to my needs.

The Way of Endurance

Though James is a passionate social critic and holds the
power structure of the social order responsible for much

of human suffering, his passion is also directed to the sufferers. In empathy he offers them the counsel to endure. This counsel is deceptively obvious. Endure? What else can one do? At best it sounds like the advice of the Stoics. Grit your teeth and bear it! But James is no Stoic. Nor is his counsel superficial. The sufferer who shrugs and says, "What else can I do but endure? What choice do I have?" is himself missing the obvious. He does not *have* to endure his suffering. He can resist it, fight it, or in other ways emotionally refuse it. He can withdraw in bitterness from others or inflict his bitterness upon them. To endure means something other than simply to suffer. This is evident from our use of the noun *endurance*. Some have more of it than others. In fact, the same person may vary in his patience from circumstance to circumstance. The Greek word for endure that James uses means literally to *remain* in contrast to running away. To endure is to persevere—to manifest *staying* power.

James' counsel to sufferers implies that they do have a choice. They may be unable *not* to suffer but they can choose their attitude toward their suffering. It was the reality of this choice that Viktor Frankl observed while he was an inmate of a Nazi concentration camp. Those who chose to persevere—to endure—the horrors of Auschwitz, for example, were more likely to survive that ordeal than those who gave up. Frankl further observed—and experienced—that it was those who held onto their belief in meaning who made the choice to endure. In his own case the memory of his wife, who he believed still lived, was the catalyst for his desire to endure. Endurance is a manifestation of strength, not of weakness. It is an affirmation, an assertion, of the acceptance of suffering. It is patience rather than resignation.

Though most of us choose to avoid suffering, some have a need for it. The escapist finds in suffering an accepted substitute for assuming his responsibilities. The masochist uses suffering to pacify guilt feelings. Suffering provides the adversity he needs to support his self-image. Endurance is something other than evasion and masochism. Rather than clinging to suffering to meet such needs, the person who endures is responding to his suffering as an end in itself. We use such colloquialisms as "hang in there" and "sweat it out" to express endurance. To endure suffering is to accept in a positive and self-affirming way what cannot be changed.

For James, endurance is based on one's confidence in the compassion and mercy of God. The sufferer is confronted by what theologians call the "hiddenness of God." Though his confidence is strained by his suffering, it is still affirmed. In this confidence the sufferer "establishes his heart." Though all understandings of meaning are stretched and even mocked by our tragedies, we may yet experience some degree of security in our spirits. Though our reasoning capacities seem bankrupted by the turn of events, we may yet find a context of meaning for our sufferings at the intuitive level of our beings. In the expansion of awareness that comes through knowing God, we may be able, at least now and then, to acknowledge him in all our ways (Prov. 3:6).

In my own experience of tragedy, I found not only that endurance is possible, but also that joy and sorrow can exist together—at the same time—in the same person.

Though God is hidden by tragedy, he is still a reality. Dismissing him as an illusion made no more sense to me than attempting to establish a meaning for the tragedy at a rational level. On the basis of a shattered yet nonetheless continuing belief in God and in the mercy of God, I was able to endure.

Endurance is not simply a way of coping with suffering; it is also an influence for personal development. Therefore James counsels us to let endurance have its full effect. Suffering in itself is no stimulus for self-development, but the way in which we cope with it can be such a stimulus. The way of endurance places us in a position to develop potentials which otherwise might remain unrealized. Therefore the full effect of endurance is our completion: the development of our potential as persons—unique persons—in relationship with God.

The Option of Scapegoating

A common alternative to endurance is to release the tensions and frustrations of suffering in an attack upon others. Oppressed people, for example, frequently attack each other as the only available outlet for their hostile feelings. Because they could not retaliate against their Egyptian overlords, the enslaved Israelites of the Old Testament found occasions to attack each other. It was in his attempt to be a peacemaker among his own people that the young Moses was rejected by them and fled from Egypt to the deserts of Midian. In our own time and country oppressed black people in their ghetto captivity have taken their frustrations out on each other in crimes of violence because of their apparent impotence before the Man.

The oppressors of modern society are often hidden in the sheer magnitude of the system. Though powerful, they are also nameless and consequently unreachable. The targets of the oppressed are usually those who, like themselves, are powerless in the system. Our anger at high prices is vented on the local manager of a chain store or even on the clerk at the check-out counter, and our frustrations over unemployment are heaped upon the personnel of the local employment office.

Because so frequently we cannot cope directly with our frustrations, we let them out indirectly on a scapegoat. The most accessible scapegoats are those who are most obviously our own people. For this reason the family takes the brunt of the attack. We exploit the acceptance that family life provides to compensate for the unacceptance we encounter in most other societal institutions. We lash out in our frustrations toward the most available family member and dump the anguish of our suffering upon this hapless substitute. Somebody has to be blamed. We cannot hit God—he is too intangible. We cannot lash the doctor—he does not need us as much as we need him. Yet the anguish of pain creates a subliminal hostility. Few of us plan to lay our frustrations on our loved ones. Rather in our anguish we impulsively lash out at the most convenient target. Some slight irritation is all that we need to justify dumping the whole load. In retrospect we see things a bit more objectively and feel guilty about the unfairness of the attack. We may even become depressed over it.

The fact that we feel guilty about the way we have

mishandled our frustrations implies an awareness that such actions are not inevitable. We could have done otherwise. Our guilt feelings also imply that our scapegoating option does not have our full approval. We find it difficult to like ourselves in that role. There ought to be a better way to cope with our suffering. There is, says James: you can *endure* your sufferings.

Options Imply Choice

If we have options in our response to suffering, we obviously have a decision to make. Because of all the predisposing factors at work in human life, freedom of choice may seem more romantic than real. We have our built-in habit patterns—our tapes and scripts—which we follow automatically if not compulsively. We are conditioned to react in the same way to the same stimuli. People who know us well may even predict our behavior.

All these influences from within and without complicate our freedom but do not eliminate it. Our own attitude toward this possibility of choice is much more crucial. If we feel helpless before these influences, we probably will be just that—helpless. What appears to be the opposite attitude, however, results in the same kind of bondage. The person who says he could do this or that if he chose to do so is exhibiting a false kind of confidence. In the former instance choice is abandoned, and in the latter it is reserved for fantasy. The person who feels helpless is not facing up to his possibility of choice; and the person who says he can but does not, is not facing up to the difficulty of choice. Both are escaping their obligation to take seriously the responsibility to change their behavior when aware of its inadequacy.

James zeroes in on both of these escapes from responsibility by accepting no substitute for *doing*. Those who say they can and don't, as well as those who say they can't and don't, are confronted. Through faith in God we have the potential: therefore actualize it! In suffering, endure!

Enduring suffering does not imply any collaboration with it that might prolong it. In itself suffering is no virtue. Whatever can be done to eliminate it should be done. We should ponder the possibility that we may have a subconscious need for our suffering or at least may be taking advantage of its secondary gains (a term used by Eric Berne to illustrate the dynamics of double-mindedness). If we are getting some advantages from our afflictions, we may hold on to them even though we also want to be rid of them. A headache, for example, has become the symbol of an excuse. "I've got a headache" means "Count me out," and without realizing it the sufferer may be reluctant to resume the responsibilities from which he has been excused.

The dissenter who suffers for his protests against social injustice is particularly susceptible to secondary gains. When someone is disgruntled with himself, he may project his anger onto society, attacking its injustices as a release for his hostility. Our unresolved rebellion against parental figures may become fixed upon all authorities symbolized by the Establishment. Some of us need excitement (this is called stimulus hunger), and attacking the culturally accepted status quo is one way of getting it.

Yet dissent and protest may also—and even at the same time—be an expression of our integrity. To eliminate our suffering by ceasing to dissent may only bring on another form of suffering. The pain of harassment is exchanged for the pain of a guilty conscience. When a person compromises his integrity in order to live harmoniously with others, he may discover he is out of harmony with himself. If enduring affliction means accepting what cannot be changed, then the suffering resulting from our protest against social injustice is accepted when in good conscience we cannot cease to protest.

Afflictions can be endured. This is a human option. But can we "count it all joy . . . when [we] meet various trials"? To the sufferer this may seem too much. Personally, I could not warm to this counsel of James. In fact, I found it a bit offensive. By no means can a sufferer count it all joy that he suffers. If he is going to be honest, he will probably say that he counts his affliction as anything but joy. Could anybody in his right mind view the experience of affliction as a happy occasion? I doubt whether even James could do so. Whatever joy there is comes not from the experience of the trials, but from what the trials produce. The crisis of pain and suffering upsets our personal world. It is possible then that out of this shake-up something new may come forth. As old patterns are broken, new ways of responding may emerge. Suffering can effect changes that might have taken much longer—or might never have come about. In this break-through of change, the sufferer has cause for joy. He does not rejoice in his affliction, but in the newness of life that his suffering has brought about.

Light at the End of the Tunnel

The problem with pain is not only its present anguish but the anxiety it creates about the future. How long will it continue? Will it *ever* go away? A psychotherapist friend of mine advises his anxious clients not to "read foreverness" into their trials. The fear about the future—that the pain will never go away—increases the anguish of the present. I recall in my own anguish phoning a friend in a distant city who several years before had experienced a similar tragedy and asking the simple question "How long does the pain last?" James offers a counteractive to this fear of the future. Rather than saying, "Don't read foreverness into your affliction," he says, "Be patient, therefore, brethren, until the coming of the Lord." There is light at the end of the tunnel. The eye of faith penetrates the frustrations of the moment to focus on this light. The Lord will come! Though the light shines from the future, it is reflected in the present.

"The coming of the Lord" is a frequent phrase in the New Testament, referring usually to the hope for the Second Coming of Christ. In contrast to his first coming, in which he identified with the sufferings of humanity, the Second Coming of Christ is a triumphant event, marking the culmination of divine deliverance from all evil. While James may have this event in mind when he refers to the coming of the Lord, he may also mean any event of divine deliverance. If we have hope in the Lord's coming to deliver us, we are inspired by that hope to endure.

This hope, says James, is like the hope of the farmer

who sows his seed and waits in patience for the early and late rains. He is trusting in the rhythm of nature which he has witnessed often enough to anticipate. Dependent upon these rains for the growth of his crop, he hopes they will come as they have before. So also the sufferer believes that God will not abandon him, but will deliver him. He has known God's mercy and compassion in the past and believes God will again reveal himself as the deliverer. He waits in patience for the coming of the Lord. His endurance of his suffering reflects his faith in God's faithfulness.

There are models for such endurance in our heritage. For an example of suffering and patience, take the prophets, who spoke in the name of the Lord. As a New Testament prophet, James points to his counterparts in the Old Covenant for his inspiration. They suffered for their dissent and protest—Micah and Jeremiah in dungeons, Elijah in exile. Yet they "hung in there"— trusting in the coming deliverance of the Lord for whom they were in trouble. His other model is Job. If the prophets' sufferings were particular, Job is the universal sufferer. Grieving over the loss of his children and of his social status, financially bankrupt and in miserable health, he longed for death. His endurance was spotty— like that of most of us. He complained, despaired, and cursed the day of his birth. Yet he also rose to heights of positive affirmation. In the midst of his agony he gave voice to his hope in the coming of the Lord:

> I know that my Redeemer lives,
>   and at last he will stand upon the earth;
> and after my skin has been thus destroyed,
>   then without [or within] my flesh I shall see God,

whom I shall see on my side,
   and my eyes shall behold, and not another. (Job 19:25-27)

Though Job never found his answer to why he had to suffer as he did, the Lord's purpose in his sufferings became clear to him. Even before his blessings were restored, he came to a realization of God's love. For James the story of Job not only reveals Job's endurance, it also reveals God's compassion and mercy. Though hidden by our afflictions, these qualities of God's Spirit are at the heart of the universe. It is possible to believe this even in tragedy. Because of this belief and the hope that it engenders, we *can* endure.

III

Toward Those Suffering—
Merciful Assistance

Religion that is pure and undefiled before God and the Father is this: to visit orphans and widows in their affliction, and to keep oneself unstained from the world. (James 1:27)

What does it profit, my brethren, if a man says he has faith but has not works? Can his faith save him? If a brother or sister is ill-clad and in lack of daily food, and one of you says to them, "Go in peace, be warmed and filled," without giving them the things needed for the body, what does it profit? So faith by itself, if it has no works, is dead. (James 2:14-17)

The socially minded Old Testament prophets were critical of any religion or religious practice that was not accompanied by charitable overtures to one's neighbor. They were critical of their own traditional religious observances because they seemed for many to be a substitute for seeking the good of one's neighbor. In particular the religious festival days with their rites of animal sacrifice drew their ire. Speaking for the Lord, Amos said:

I hate, I despise your feasts,
  and I take no delight in your solemn assemblies.
Even though you offer me your burnt
      offerings and cereal offerings,
  I will not accept them,
and the peace offerings of your fatted beasts
  I will not look upon.
Take away from me the noise of your songs;
  to the melody of your harps I will not listen.
But let justice roll down like waters,
  and righteousness like an everflowing stream.

(Amos 5:21-24)

The practice of fasting was also an object of prophetic scorn. Isaiah warned:

Fasting like yours this day
  will not make your voice to be heard on high.
Is such the fast that I choose,
  a day for a man to humble himself?
Is it to bow down his head like a rush,
  and to spread sackcloth and ashes under him?
Will you call this a fast,
  and a day acceptable to the Lord? (Isa. 58:4-5)

The prophet answers his rhetorical question by describing the true fast:

Is this not the fast that I choose:
  to loose the bonds of wickedness,
  to undo the thongs of the yoke,
to let the oppressed go free,
  and to break every yoke?
Is it not to share your bread with the hungry,
  and bring the homeless poor into your house;
when you see the naked, to cover him,
  and not to hide yourself from your own flesh? (Vv. 6-7)

51

James gives a similar description of the true fast, although he labels it *pure religion:* "Religion that is pure and undefiled before God and the Father is this: to visit orphans and widows in their affliction, and to keep oneself unstained from the world." Obviously this is not a definition of religion: there is no reference to the worship of God or to the transcendent dimensions of life or even to religious experience. Rather it is a description of the religious outreach to one's neighbor. Pure religion shows itself in caring for those who are hurting.

As we have seen, James' counsel to sufferers is to endure. But sufferers do not live as isolated individuals; they are persons in community. They need assistance from this community to endure. Pure religion is demonstrated when people offer this support—when they "visit orphans and widows in their affliction."

Pure Religion as Visitation

The orphans and widows in the Letter of James represent people who have been deprived by death of very significant persons in their lives. They are the bereaved. People bereft of a significant relationship need other relationships to mitigate the loss. Because they have been hurt by their loss, they seldom have enough ego-strength to take the initiative in seeking these other relationships. Consequently those who know them— their friends, neighbors, and acquaintances at church and at work—will have to take this initiative. They need to reach out—tangibly—to the sufferer.

In our own bereavement we appreciated the people who took this initiative, some of them once, others again and again. We also felt we understood those who did not.

We too had failed at times to take the initiative ourselves with other hurting acquaintances. We talked ourselves out of it by saying, "I wouldn't know what to say," or, "They probably want to be alone," or, "I might be calling at the wrong time." Actually we fear to take the initiative. The thought of being with the hurting person is disturbing; the actual visit threatens to be even more so. Therefore, we rationalize our way out of it. Yet there are some who brave the pain and make contact. We knew, for example, that it took courage for some people to call on us. We felt their discomfort. Yet we were grateful to them and would agree that theirs was an overture in pure religion. The value of offering our persons to those who are hurting far outweighs the reasons we give to ourselves for not taking this initiative.

The orphans and widows also represent vulnerable people. In those days they lacked the protection of a family, and in particular of the male leader of the family. They needed assistance from those who had this protection. In our day these persons are still socially vulnerable. Children of single-parent families—of mothers receiving Aid to Dependent Children, for example—may grow up without the influence of a significant male figure. We can compare the widows of James' day to the lonely senior citizens of our own day. These are the forgotten people of our society. Many of them live in high-rise apartments in the inner city or in homes for the elderly, and have little to give meaning to their lives. Their telephones rarely ring, and their rooms seldom contain visitors. The television and, in increasing instances, alcohol are poor substitutes for a living presence.

Pure religion, for James, means having compassion on hurting people such as deprived youngsters and forsaken senior citizens. It means reaching out with our persons in tangible contact. Many of us experience our most grievous sense of inferiority over our *persons.* If we do not feel confident about what to say or what to do, we can feel totally inadequate; just our *being* is not enough. The faith of our Lord Jesus Christ, which to James is the basis of pure religion, is faith regarding the justification of our naked persons—without the adornments of competency in speech and action.

Our tangible presence is of great value and worth. We need to believe this because it is true. Then we can take the leap of faith and offer our presence to those who are hurting. What we say when we "visit orphans and widows in their affliction" is of value also. In this venture, as in others, we improve by doing. Our sensitivity grows with experience. The best we can hope for is that what we say reflects who we are, and it is who we are—our person—that is basic for all communication.

Sharing More than Words

Reaching out to those who are hurting may mean more than sharing our persons or even our words; it may mean sharing also of our possessions and privileges. For example, if a person is suffering the pangs of hunger, it may raise his morale a bit to talk about it, but the exchange will be of little value ultimately if he does not get food. This is the example James uses to illustrate his polemical position on the relationship between faith and works: "If a brother or sister is ill-clad and in lack of daily food, and one of you says to them, 'Go in peace, be warmed and filled,' without giving them the things needed for the body, what does it profit?" People who are able to give us material support when we need it, or have "clout" they could use to get us a job when we are down and out, or are in a position to open other needed doors for us, but who instead are satisfied to listen to our needs—to let us "get it off our chest"—demonstrate an appalling lack of compassion. "What does it profit, my brethren, if a man says he has faith but has not works?"

Substituting words for action is what is now known as rhetoric. A political commentator stated, "The public is very sensitive to the gap between words and acts." What is needed, he said, is "straight talk." Exploited groups in particular have suffered from this gap, and they were sensitive to it long before the general public. They have heard the rhetoric many times. Blacks have heard the Man say again and again, "I believe you should have equal rights." The words are meaningless, because the implicit qualification is "not if it means I have to share any of *my* rights." The same line is heard by other deprived people: "I believe that social injustices should be rectified (but not in my neighborhood, place of work, or church)."

Rhetoric not only substitutes for action but in effect solidifies inaction. We indulge in it to play tricks on others, and, perhaps, even on ourselves. We use it to give the impression that needs will be met, and therefore conflict reduced, when in reality nothing will be done. There seems to be an element of self-justification in rhetoric—that there is some value in just saying the right words. There is less pressure, then, to do the right things. The prophetic judgment on rhetoric is not only that someone who could do good has done nothing, but that in doing nothing he has actually obstructed the good.

The church also comes under this judgment. Too often it has proclaimed its care and concern in the abstract. Care for those who are hurting becomes controversial when it is concretized. "Straight talk" tends to be abrasive when it threatens our vested interests. Who can be against motherhood in the abstract? Certainly not church people! Who can be against welfare mothers? Probably a lot of church people! Who can be hostile toward the poor in the abstract? But when the poor are labeled as the people on welfare, living on our tax money, the hostility comes forth.

The church's indulgence in rhetoric has made it necessary for many needs to be met outside the church. The poor on welfare, especially the white poor, are rarely associated with any church except what are pejoratively called "The Sects." The racism of the white church has left the segregated black churches to care for the black poor. In addition, the Black Muslims have come into being to meet the needs of poor blacks. People with drinking problems have usually received more judgment than compassion from Christian congregations. Fortunately Alcoholics Anonymous, with a theology similar to that of the church but with a different sort of fellowship, has emerged to help the alcoholic. Now homosexuals are forming their own churches because they feel not only judgment but outright exclusion from many churches.

Reaching Out Is Faith in Action

It was precisely the lack of concrete caring on the part of supposedly Christian persons and congregations that moved James to his subsequently controversial attack on the sufficiency of faith alone for salvation. Reaching out—tangibly—to persons in need in an effort to meet their needs is an expression of one's faith. Historically the prophet's ire has been aroused against religious substitutes for such reaching out. In Old Testament times the people distorted the use of religious ritual for this purpose. For the New Testament prophet this distortion is in the misuse of religious dogma: "What does it profit, my brethren, if a man says he has faith but has not works? Can his faith save him?"

The New Testament doctrine of justification by faith is spelled out clearly by Paul in his Letter to the Romans: "For we hold that a man is justified by faith apart from works of law" (Rom. 3:28); "Therefore, since we are justified by faith, we have peace with God through our Lord Jesus Christ" (Rom. 5:1). Some early Christians among James' acquaintances were evidently distorting this doctrine, saying that since we are justified by our faith, works are no longer necessary. Against this distortion James raises his prophetic protest, "Show me your faith apart from your works, and I by my works will show you my faith" (2:18).

This apparent attack, within the biblical canon, against justification by faith was a source of irritation to Martin Luther in his conflict with the papacy over this very doctrine. In comparison with the Letters of Paul and I Peter, he termed the Letter of James a "straw epistle." He is quoted as expressing himself even more strongly in his Table Talk: "Today or tomorrow I will set a bright fire with little Jim." Another Table comment is equally caustic: "The Epistle of James is written by a Jew who so far as Christianity is concerned has indeed heard the bell ring, but does not know where the clapper is. Here in Wittenberg we have cast James out of theology: indeed we have almost thrown him out of the Bible."

Extreme words! Yet James too can sound extreme. Pointing to the example of the Old Testament patriarch Abraham's willingness to offer up his son, he says, "You see that a man is justified by works and not by faith alone" (2:24). In the polemics of the Reformation, this statement seems to put James squarely on the side of Luther's ecclesiastical opponents. When I read this section from James at our family devotional time, my Lutheran-oriented son was aghast. To him James was undermining the security of faith. "Those words take away the one hope of the frail," he said.

These words were not meant for the frail, however. Imagine for a moment the situation that must have been confronting James. He was evidently facing opposition to his prophetic appeal for compassion, from Christians who were using the doctrine of justification by faith as an argument. Faith as a substitute for compassion! James offers an unequivocal "Never!"

Although the epistle makes no mention of Paul, Luther interpreted James' attack on faith without works as opposition to Paul. "I will give my doctor's beret as a gift to anyone who can bring Paul and James into agreement," he is quoted as saying. Once we leave the polemical atmosphere of the Reformation, however, it can be shown that James' explicit conflict is not with Paul, but rather with a distortion of Paul's teaching. People who used the doctrine of justification by faith to justify their lack of compassion would get no support from Paul, who spoke of "faith working through love" (Gal. 5:16). Though he probably did not write the Letter to Titus, his name was attached to it because it represented his teachings. In this letter we read that those who believe in God should be "careful to apply themselves to good deeds" (Tit. 3:8).

The key to solving the apparent conflict centers in the words "faith without works." Using James' own analogy we can say that faith without works is no more faith than a dead body is a person. "For as the body apart from the spirit is dead, so faith apart from works is dead" (2:26). It is obvious from his own context what James means by works. He has been dwelling upon meeting the needs of the destitute—the widows, the orphans, the poor—in a tangible way. No claim to faith can substitute for such reaching out to the needy. Works, therefore, are deeds of mercy, of compassion.

If a man says he has faith but has not works, can his faith save him? To make his point James speaks in extremes. It may be difficult to conceive of someone whose life exhibits no works, but what James means, obviously, is one who is decidedly lacking in good works—lacking in acts of mercy and compassion. To some degree and at certain times, I suppose, this indictment fits all of us. We probably have had those occasions when we exhibited more of the appearance, the rhetoric, than the essence, the action, of compassion. We too know what it is to become so preoccupied with our own needs or with the fear of involvement that we fail to respond to, or perhaps even to hear, the cry for help from a neighbor. But we are probably repentant about these times. It is to be hoped that they are aberrations in our life-style rather than a description of it. If, however, we were to attempt to defend our inadequacy in showing mercy by contending that such works are not really necessary since we are justified by faith, we would place ourselves under the prophetic indictment.

Luther's opinion notwithstanding, James does not "talk nonsense." Claiming faith as a substitute for mercy is tantamount to the death of faith. "The kingdom of God," says Paul, "does not consist in talk but in power" (I Cor. 4:20). Rhetoric is no substitute for action. The civil rights movement expressed it in the positive: Put your body with your words! Jesus set his disciples straight on precisely this issue. They had discovered a stranger in the act of exorcising the demon-possessed in Jesus' name. In relating the event to Jesus, they said, "We forbade him, because he was not following us." He did not have the right label or associate with the right company. The Master cut through the pettiness. "Do not forbid him," he said; "for no one who does a mighty work in my name will be able soon after to speak evil of me" (Mark 9:38, 40).

By unequivocally stating that a work of mercy has no need of an accompanying defense, Jesus was giving expression to his own style of living. In all four of the Gospels, his motivation for healing the sick, restoring sight to the blind, feeding the hungry, reviving the dead, and preaching the Good News to the poor, is ascribed to compassion: "And when the Lord saw her, he had compassion on her"; "Then Jesus called his disciples to him and said, 'I have compassion on the crowd'" (Luke 7:13; Matt. 15:32).

The Greek word for compassion comes from the word

for bowels or intestines. Literally it means "to be moved in one's viscera." The ancient Hebrews thought symbolically of the bowels or intestines as the seat of human affection and compassion. In this sense the figure is in line with our contemporary expression "gut-level" to indicate genuine caring and honest feelings. The hurts and needs of others are the stimuli for compassion. Our faith in Christ moves us to respond to these needs in tangible terms. The logic is obvious: those who are the recipients of mercy, who share in the faith of our Lord Jesus Christ, are those most likely to respond in mercy.

Developing Our Sensitivity

I have a clergyman friend who has an amazing insight into the feelings of others. He "picks up" depression or hurt which is otherwise successfully hidden behind a facade. My friend refers to his ability as a gift, and while I am sure that his perceptiveness is a gift, I believe that it is a gift that more of us could have. The potential for sensitivity is a gift that goes with our humanity. The *development* of this potential is a matter of discipline and exercise. My friend has trained himself to listen to his own feelings, and when he is with others he consciously exercises his sensitivity to the total, not just the verbal, communication. On the basis of this "total" listening he reaches out to assist (unlike some, he does not hesitate to act).

The fact that we become sensitive to the feelings of others through listening to our own feelings shows how much we share a common humanity. It is not that some of us are dependent and others are independent but that all of us are interdependent. The giver is also the receiver.

The one who reaches out to assist today may tomorrow need someone to reach out to him. If he is sensitive to his own feelings, he will probably be open enough to respond to assistance when it is offered to him.

Some people who are eager enough to reach out are meeting primarily their own needs rather than those of the other person. Their need to be a helper interferes with their sensitivity to the other's feelings. Most of us have at some time or other shrunk back almost in fright from the overtures of someone "determined" to help us. I once listened as a young wife told her husband, in a voice shaken by both sorrow and anger, how much she could have done for him to help him establish himself successfully, but instead he had been unresponsive to her efforts. She had projected onto him her own idea of what he needed from her rather than being sensitive to how he perceived his needs. Quite obviously her efforts to "help" him had turned him off. Yet he had needs, plenty of them, which she could have helped to satisfy had she been sufficiently open.

James' approach is quite different: visit, get involved, give yourself, listen! Then give the needed assistance. It is not that simple, however. In spite of the danger of deciding in our own minds what other people need from us, we cannot assume that they themselves are able to assess their needs accurately. An alcoholic is quite sure he needs more alcohol, yet if we really care about him we must not give him alcohol. Not everything that pleases people is helpful to them. "Give the rich, to please them, riches" (*The Love Letters of Phyllis McGinley* [New York: Viking Press, 1954], p. 7).

What is the difference, then, between projecting our

own agenda onto others and refusing to give them what they ask of us? Though these two courses of action appear similar on the surface, there can be a big difference between them. Projecting our agenda on another may be a way of controlling, possessing, the other, whereas refusing to give him what pleases him may be a way of caring for him. How can we know whether our course of action is really showing care for another? As limited human beings we probably can never be absolutely sure. But we can come close. It requires more than the motivation of compassion and the capacity for sensitivity; it also requires *knowledge*. This knowledge comes from an understanding of ourselves, of human nature, and of the ways of health and happiness. The ancients called this wisdom.

IV

Wisdom from Above

If any of you lacks wisdom, let him ask God, who gives to all men generously and without reproaching, and it will be given him. (James 1:5)

Who is wise and understanding among you? By his good life let him show his works in the meekness of wisdom. But if you have bitter jealousy and selfish ambition in your hearts, do not boast and be false to the truth. This wisdom is not such as comes down from above, but is earthly, unspiritual, devilish. For where jealousy and selfish ambition exist, there will be disorder and every vile practice. But the wisdom from above is first pure, then peaceable, gentle, open to reason, full of mercy and good fruits, without uncertainty or insincerity. And the harvest of righteousness is sown in peace by those who make peace. (James 3:13-18)

"Get wisdom: and with all thy getting get understanding" (Prov. 4:7 KJV). The Old Testament has several odes and other tributes to wisdom, and James with his Old Testament roots considers it a prime possession. Wisdom is a kind of knowledge—basically a knowledge of life. It includes a knowledge of oneself, of personal relationships, of life in community, and of human fulfillment. What wisdom one possesses centers in a context of values, priorities, insights; it provides the evaluative potential to meet one's constant need to make decisions.

An Intuitive Level of Knowing

We can take courses in universities, or practical workshops in other institutions, which teach the data of the sciences of human nature and human society. Psychology, sociology, and anthropology can all assist us in the development of wisdom; in fact one psychology book is entitled *The Science of Living.* Yet wisdom is something other than a knowledge of these sciences. Formal education can foster wisdom but cannot guarantee it.

Wisdom may be a long time in developing. "So soon old, so late smart." As André Malraux has observed, "It may take one sixty years of incredible suffering and effort to achieve wisdom, and then he is good only for dying." Yet if the person is really wise, he will not be cynical about life or about death. He will also realize that the knowledge that he has obtained has not come just because he is sixty years of age. Surrounded by older people who obviously have not learned very much from their many experiences, he knows that one may be an *old* fool as well as an *educated* fool.

The irony of a lack of wisdom is that this sort of knowledge should come to one naturally. Eric Berne says that we accumulate it quickly and then lose it, so that all subsequent development in wisdom is merely a recovery process. According to Berne, the human being exits in three ego states, the Parent, the Child, and the Adult. In a second order of this structure the Child ego state has its own Parent, Child, and Adult components. The Adult is called "the little professor" because of his keen and perceptive knowledge of human nature. "In fact," writes Berne in *What Do You Say After You Say Hello?* "he knows more practical psychology and psychiatry than any grownup professor does, although after many years of training and experience, a grownup professor may know as much as thirty-five percent of what he knew when he was four years old" (New York: Bantam Books, 1973 [p. 104]).

While Berne may write statements like the above tongue in cheek, the "little professor" is nevertheless a "sharpee" in intuitive understanding. All human beings are created with the potential for awareness of what is going on in their own psyches and in their transactions with others. Though rationally the child is not yet able to reflect or to conceptualize, his intuitive awareness provides the basis for the development of wisdom.

The Development of Blinders

Something happens, universally, to disrupt the development of wisdom in human beings. Our early perceptive awarenesses tend to become dulled behind blinders and earplugs. Berne lays the blame for this discontinuity on parents or parental figures, who in turn contribute to the development of a similar Parent ego state in the child. Other analysts—Otto Rank, for example—are more existentially oriented and place the problem in the life-against-death nature of human existence. As a being who becomes conscious of his own vulnerability and mortality, the human child defends himself against this awareness by repressing it. The human dilemma is that we seemingly cannot bear the full brunt of knowing what it means to be a human being. The termination of all life in death, together with all the symbols of negativity related to death, is too much to tolerate.

The repression of this intolerable awareness does not eliminate the anxiety that it provokes, however. In fact, this anxiety may become basic to our personality dynamics. Karen Horney describes its content as the feeling that one is alone and vulnerable in the midst of a hostile universe. The mechanics of denial and repression are learned in early life as a means for survival. What Kierkegaard calls a self-imposed ignorance seems necessary to hold the self together. Since the capacity for knowledge becomes the means for making life intolerable, the human being is evidently equipped to screen out the threatening aspects of this knowledge in order to function with a degree of efficiency and equanimity.

Consequently, as Kierkegaard observed, it is possible in growing older to go *from* something as well as *to* something. The intuitive knowledge of the "little professor" diminishes as one leaves childhood. In adolescence, however, there is often a breakthrough of the repressed knowledge (young people's insights into human values are usually upsetting to their elders). As the responsibilities of adulthood increase, these insights into the nature of life again become intolerable and are once more screened out as a way of survival. For this reason, as the sages have often observed, aging and wisdom do not necessarily go together.

The Old Testament character Job, to whom James later refers, was visited by four friends, who came to comfort and condole with him in his suffering. The fourth friend, Elihu, was considerably younger than the other three and, because of the cultural deference to age, was obliged to wait until his elders had had their say. When the three older ones were frustrated by Job's bitter protest of his suffering, Elihu became angry. The halo of the aged was wearing thin, and when the three finally gave up and ceased to answer Job, Elihu had his opportunity. Before passing on his own counsel to Job, he vented his disillusion with his elders:

> I said, "Let days speak,
>   and many years teach wisdom."
> But it is the spirit in a man,
>   the breath of the Almighty,
>   that makes him understand.
> It is not the old that are wise,
>   nor the aged that understand what is right. (Job 32:7-9)

Surely the increase of years should bring with it an increase in knowledge; but defensive habits well entrenched by years of repetition disrupt the expected progression. The investment in these defenses increases with the years, and the tenacity with which one can hold to them, as illustrated by Job's three friends, shows their relationship to self-preservation.

Still, there is something very *un*wise about a purely defensive stance toward life. Jesus alluded to this when he said that those who seek to save their lives will lose them (Matt. 16:25). So much may be screened out for our protection that the resulting limitation upon our consciousness stultifies our development. Because the web of illusions that we spin to protect ourselves from the painful reality of ourselves and of life is ominously fragile, we attempt to keep it intact by distractions that fix our attention. Because we need these distractions in order to maintain the tenuous balance with illusion, we can become addicted to them. The addiction itself may then become the problem. The kinds of distractions that we are addicted to vary with the individual. For some of us a shopping spree will suffice. Others of us devote ourselves to work. Still others choose to ingest chemicals to drug their sensitivities. The most common and most dangerous of these drugs is alcohol.

The consequences of some addictions are culturally perceived as more devastating than others. The work addict, for example, is contributing to the productivity of a production-oriented society, regardless of the harm his addiction may be doing to his health or his marraige or his social adjustment. In contrast the alcoholic is unable to function efficiently in his work and is generally a greater hazard to society because of his impaired rational and motor controls. The subsequent crisis of alcoholism has led to several treatment programs, the most successful and well known of which is Alcoholics Anonymous.

The AA program consists of twelve steps, the fourth and fifth of which form the structure of the treatment programs in most chemical-dependency treatment centers. These steps are an antidote to the addict's penchant for evasion. In contrast to the screening-out processes of repression, the fourth step directs the addict to "make a searching and fearless moral inventory of himself." To be effective, this inventory needs to be shared, and so the fourth step leads to the fifth: "Admit to God, to ourselves and to another person, the exact nature of our wrongs." This step is an exercise in the breaking down of defenses and in the cultivation of honesty.

As is implicit in the fifth step, the clarity of vision to which the alcoholic returns is basically a religious perspective. This perspective is spelled out in the second step: "Come to believe that a Power greater than our own selves could restore us to sanity." (We could paraphrase this step as a restoration to wisdom.) The third step builds on the second: "Make a decision to turn our will and our lives over to the care of God as we understand him." This step is based on a specific insight into the nature of man—namely, that he needs to align himself with that which is over and beyond himself in order to relate positively to himself. As a creature he has a need to give himself, not just to another creature or to his own creative handiwork, but to the Creator. This understanding of man is itself wisdom; in fact the Old Testament identifies it as the beginning of wisdom.

Love at the Core of the Universe

"The fear of the Lord is the beginning of wisdom" (Prov. 9:10). The word *fear* in "fear of the Lord" does not mean "to be afraid of," but rather is the word used for "respect" when applied to God. The parallel or complementary clause to this proverb is "and the knowledge of the Holy One is insight." In other words, if a person respects God—recognizes him as God—he gains insight into a dimension beyond the obvious dimensions of his human existence. In this sense he transcends these human dimensions and in so doing places them within a particular view of meaning and purpose. His knowledge, consequently, is inseparable from his faith, his understanding inseparable from his belief. "Understanding," said St. Augustine, "is the reward of faith. Therefore seek not to understand that thou mayest believe, but believe that thou mayest understand." He who so understands remains a part of the world of nature, bound by its limits, and he also transcends them through his identification by faith with the Reality that is over and beyond this world.

Knowledge in itself can be too great a burden to endure if one has no belief that transcends the limits of human understanding and endeavor. As Ernest Becker states, "If repression makes an untenable life liveable, self-knowledge can entirely destroy it for some people" (*The Denial of Death* [New York: Free Press, 1973], p. 269). If we are to be constructive and creative in our living, we need a way to transcend the limitations of human existence—limits which can be very frightening as well as depressing, for they suppress, even disintegrate, our identity. Any meaningful context for knowledge will of necessity be required not only to incorporate the realities of death and all related experiences, but also to do so *positively*. The evidence from human experience is clear that human beings as self-conscious entities cannot be satisfied with the limitations which so decisively limit all forms of nature. A context of meaning sufficient for persons, obviously, must transcend these arbitrary limits. Faith has been called a leap because it leaps across these otherwise impenetrable boundaries.

The nearest thing to a patron saint of AA is the prodigal son who wasted his inheritance in riotous living. He is also an example of *un*wisdom. After pressuring his father to give him his share of the inheritance while the father was still alive, he showed his unreadiness to receive it by spending it in ways destructive to his own identity. Penniless and far from home, he took the only job open to him—one abhorrent to a Hebrew—swine feeder. He was too desperate to be proud, however, and would even have eaten the swine's food to ease his hunger pains, but he was forbidden by his employer to do so. Then it was that he "came to himself." In AA terms, he "hit bottom." The New English Bible has "He came to his senses." His wisdom restored, his defenses gone, he saw clearly, intuitively, into reality. He knew then what to do; he would go to his father.

The father in this parable represents God, and the prodigal a human being who, though a son of God, has lost his way. In deciding to return to his father, he was in effect making "a decision to turn his life over to the care of God." In coming to himself he became aware that love—not hostility—is at the core of the universe. The anxiety that Horney perceives in disturbed persons is due to their own self-rejection which they project onto the universe. They have become lost in wandering far from home—from their basic identity.

The Meekness of Wisdom

Because James understands wisdom as knowledge based on the fear of the Lord, he refers to it as "the wisdom from above" and "the meekness of wisdom." These two descriptions are directly related. The word *meek* connotes its original meaning, namely, kind, gentle. Its opposite is *arrogant, harsh*. The wisdom from above is meek toward others. The reason is obvious. Those who receive the wisdom from above know they are *under* God and not *as* God. In other words, they can accept their own creatureliness. Consequently they are not driven to be something other than what they are. Without this perspective, wisdom ceases to be the meekness of wisdom and degenerates into "knowledge," which "puffs up" (I Cor. 8:1).

The conceit which knowledge may breed is itself an obstacle to knowledge. Those who consider themselves authorities may tend arbitrarily to limit its boundaries. The experience of the explorers Krapf and Rebmann, who discovered Mount Kilimanjaro for the Western world, is one example among many of this arbitrariness. They were not believed by certain scientists when they described the mountain as snow-capped. The reason: it was too close to the equator for snow. So whether it has snow or not (it has), it cannot have snow, because our knowledge says it is too close to the equator. The commonness of such closed-mindedness among so-called knowledgeable persons has moved someone to quip that the prime law of academia is "Never try anything for the first time."

The phrase "meekness of wisdom" reflects a particular view of authority. The person who is meek is willing to ask as well as to answer. His exercise of whatever authority he possesses is different from that of one who views his authority as an authority over others. James is particularly conscious of this differentiation in authority as it pertains to the position of teaching. Among the early Christians the teacher held a position not unlike that of the Jewish rabbi in dignity and respect. James considers himself such a teacher.

As the dispenser of knowledge, the teacher has a particularly risky vocation. "For you know that we who teach shall be judged with greater strictness" (James 3:1). It is easy to slip from a partnership with students in the pursuit of knowledge to become the lonely authority who possesses this knowledge. I have known both of these stances in my years as a teacher. Since the tragedy in my life I have felt myself to be something other than an authority in knowledge. Consequently I have changed the format of my teaching from standing behind a podium speaking words of wisdom to students sitting in rows before me to joining the students in a circle of chairs. This arrangement of the classroom expresses my own view of authority, in which both teacher and students participate in the mutuality of giving and receiving. One who occupies a position of authority is open to the temptation to enter the illusory world of the authoritarian, in which he erects boundaries to knowledge where no boundaries actually exist.

Wisdom that loses its meekness is for James no longer the wisdom from above but wisdom of the earth. This is the knowledge that lacks the transcendent dimension and, confined to limitations of human existence, becomes distorted by them. Under the domination of death, the wisdom of the earthbound is corrupted by "jealousy and selfish ambition." As such it forms the basic mind-set of our competitive value system. Under its influence each is pitted against his neighbor in a struggle for a bigger share of the pie. Even the groups with which one is associated become means for his own self-aggrandizement. Hiding his motivations lest his behavior be too obvious, he finds it hard to trust others, since he suspects them of similar motivations. The strife, factions, and alienation that ensue demonstrate both the tragedy and the stupidity of earthly wisdom, whose values and priorities prevent the very cooperation necessary for human community. The corruption of the human spirit that follows constitutes "the world's stain," which we shall discuss in greater detail in a later chapter.

The wisdom from above is a contrast to earthly wisdom in every way. It is known by its peaceableness, gentleness, openness to reason, clarity, congruity, and compassion. There is nothing to hide in this wisdom, because it is first of all *pure*. It cannot be mixed with earthly wisdom without completely changing its essence. Unlike earthly wisdom it contains no hidden agendas: it is open and clear. There is no confusion over who is God and who is creature. The *meekness* of wisdom is genuine. Its purity leads to its peaceableness. "Be still and receive from above, and know that I—not you or they—am God," to paraphrase Psalm 46:10.

How is it, then, that those who should possess this wisdom may at times demonstrate also the qualities of earthly wisdom? People who believe in God—you and I, perhaps—become victims of jealousy and selfish ambition with the resultant strife and alienation. At the time of this writing an entire church denomination is polarized by strife, seemingly exhibiting all the qualities of earthly wisdom. Pettiness as well as ruthlessness has characterized its power struggle, much to the delight of a sensationally minded press.

Unfortunately this situation is not unusual in the history of Christendom. How come? Obviously the answer is that in spite of our desire for the wisdom from above we also participate in earthly wisdom. We are a "fallen humanity," and institutions, including the church, and people, including Christians, are not immune. James faces the problem directly: "If you have bitter jealousy and selfish ambition in your hearts, do not boast or be false to the truth." If you are guilty of exhibiting the qualities of earthly wisdom, do not deny, rationalize, spiritualize, or in any other way defend or exonerate yourselves. Instead, recognize the fact that *this* wisdom is not such as comes from above. Such recognition is in itself a manifestation of the wisdom from above. It is the first step in effecting change. "Who is wise and understanding among you? By his good life let him show his works in the meekness of wisdom." The ultimate test is our attitude and behavior toward others.

Ask for It

"Enough of all these descriptions," you may say. "I know I lack wisdom. So what else is new? But how do I get it?" James is exasperatingly simple on this point: if you lack it, since it is the wisdom from above, ask God for it.

Asking as a way of receiving wisdom is an old biblical theme. There is, for example, the story of how the king noted for his wisdom obtained it. When Solomon became king of Israel, succeeding his father David, he had a dream in which God appeared to him and said, "Ask what

I shall give you." Feeling the burden of his new responsibilities, Solomon asked for wisdom because, he said, "Who is able to govern this thy great people?" (I Kings 3:9).

There is also the story of how Jesus became separated from his parents on their journey to Jerusalem and was later found by them in the temple. He was sitting among the teachers, listening to them and asking them questions, and the teachers were amazed at his understanding. He was twelve years old at the time and was described as growing in wisdom as well as in stature. Asking as a way of receiving is also advocated in the familiar words from the Sermon on the Mount: "Ask, and it will be given you: seek, and you will find; knock, and it will be opened to you" (Matt. 7:7).

James encourages his readers to ask for wisdom, on the assurance that God "gives to all men generously and without reproaching" (1:5). Some people are afraid to ask, for fear of censure. A student may ask a teacher a question and be made to feel stupid for having asked it. Some students refrain from asking because they fear a put-down, either from the teacher or from their classmates, and need encouragement to ask, lest their means of protection against humiliation stifle their development in knowledge. Asking is a risk we can afford to take—and cannot afford *not* to take. Otherwise our defensive stance will lead eventually to the blinders and the earplugs. God does not upbraid the asker.

Risking goes with learning. We risk by asking, by venturing, by becoming involved, by trying. We can, of course, risk ourselves foolishly. But again, how do we determine what is foolish? By asking, by trying, by listening, and by receiving. Asking God for wisdom implies being receptive to his answer. When we ask God we are in effect asking life. We can learn from our experience, even from our mistakes and failures. Or perhaps I should say, *especially* through our mistakes and failures. This may be because we tend to dwell on our mistakes and failures. I believe we could learn even more from our accuracies and our successes if we were as prone to reflect upon them as we are upon our failures.

Even though we are preoccupied with our failures, we may still not receive much wisdom from them. This is because we may so magnify the failure that it depresses us. We upbraid *ourselves* to such an extent that we undermine our confidence. This is most likely to happen when our asking is corrupted by earthly wisdom so that we identify our achievements with our persons. Then if someone fails in an activity, he has failed as a person. The self-beratement that follows may so devastate his initiative that he fears to risk himself again, and thereby frustrates the process through which he could receive wisdom.

The Power that is higher than ourselves does not upbraid those who ask. Love and not hostility is at the core of the universe. There is no need to protect ourselves from judgment upon our ventures. We are liberated by God, who gives generously to all that we may receive and accept evaluation. The God who does not upbraid is also the God who forgives, and through his forgiveness we can forgive ourselves, even our failures, and in reflecting upon the experience can venture forth again with increased wisdom.

V

The Obstacle of Double-Mindedness

Let him ask in faith, with no doubting, for he who doubts is like a wave of the sea that is driven and tossed by the wind. For that person must not suppose that a double-minded man, unstable in all his ways, will receive anything from the Lord. (James 1:6-8)

You desire and do not have; so you kill. And you covet and cannot obtain; so you fight and wage war. You do not have, because you do not ask. You ask and do not receive, because you ask wrongly, to spend it on your passions. Unfaithful creatures! Do you not know that friendship with the world is enmity with God? Therefore whoever wishes to be a friend of the world makes himself an enemy of God. Or do you suppose it is in vain that the scripture says, "He yearns jealously over the spirit which he has made to dwell in us"? But he gives more grace; therefore it says, "God opposes the proud, but gives grace to the humble." Submit yourselves therefore to God. Resist the devil and he will flee from you. Draw near to God and he will draw near to you. Cleanse your hands, you sinners, and purify your hearts, you men of double mind. Be wretched and mourn and weep. Let your laughter be turned to mourning and your joy to dejection. Humble yourselves before the Lord and he will exalt you. (James 4:2-10)

Asking as a way to receive needs qualification. It is one thing to ask; it may be another to ask *in faith.* "Let him ask in faith, with no doubting, for he who doubts is like a wave of the sea that is driven and tossed by the wind."

Two Kinds of Doubt

There are two kinds of doubt. One is intellectual doubt—a natural concomitant of faith. This kind of doubt is implied in our use of the word *faith* in contrast to *knowledge.* When something is verifiable in a sensory and rational way, we speak of it as *fact.* But not everything of worth is verifiable in this tangible way. Values, meaning, and purpose in life are not solely the domain of science. Rather these are religious entities. The shadows are present, and the unknown persists, providing a legitimate basis for doubt; but one can act—take the leap of faith—in spite of these obstacles.

The other kind of doubt actually prevents such a leap. This is self-doubt, which divides a person so that he cannot act. He has, in fact, a double mind and is programmed to defeat by his doubt. He is beat before he begins. Rather than existing in a natural tension with faith, this kind of doubt is faith's opposite, since it focuses in the will. To doubt in this sense means to be at variance, hesitant within oneself. It is the opposite of decision. "She doesn't know what she wants" describes such a doubter. Or "He can't get his head together"; "He can't make up his mind"; "He is only partially in what he is doing." This is the kind of doubt to which James refers.

Such a person is not in a state of mind to receive—even what he supposedly asks for or desires. He is driven and tossed by opposing forces like a wave of the sea because he lacks self-direction. His doubting sabotages his efforts and blocks his receiving. "For that person must not suppose that a double-minded man, unstable in all his ways, will receive anything from the Lord."

Double-Mindedness as Ambivalence

As a contrast to single-mindedness, the condition of double-mindedness implies that the person has two opposing minds, one of which is frequently hidden and unacknowledged. In his *Confessions*, Augustine contemplated this inability of human beings to direct themselves and deemed it most mysterious. How is it, he asked, that the mind can tell the body what to do—such as to raise the hand—and the body immediately obeys. Yet the mind can tell the mind what to do and nothing may happen. Surely the mind is closer to itself than it is to the body! Whence comes this mysterious phenomenon? His conclusion is that it really isn't so mysterious after all. In reality there are two minds rather than one, "and what the one hath, the other lacketh."

The psychological term for this double-mindedness is *ambivalence*, which means literally "conflicting *wills*." The double-minded person is unstable because his will is divided. Like the people of Israel who wanted to enter the Promised Land and yet feared to do so, the double-minded person is stymied by this conflict. He "wanders in the wilderness" as did they, rather than heading in one direction or another. When this double-mindedness continued to characterize the Israelites even after they had occupied the Promised Land, the prophet

81

Elijah asked, "How long will you go limping with two different opinions?" (I Kings 18:21).

Causes of Double-Mindedness

Fear

A major cause of double-mindedness is obviously fear. I ask for what I want, but I also want to be safe. Frightened by the prospect of actually entering the Promised Land, the people of Israel began to exaggerate the risks: there were *giants* in the land. Gripped by anxiety, the Israelites became immobilized.

Fear divides us. In social situations, for example, we become self-conscious. Fear inhibits our efforts and even our speech. We become awkward and unspontaneous, unable, it seems, to direct ourselves. Our attention is divided between the precariousness of our existence and the situation at hand. The result is a painful disintegration.

As the opposite of self-doubt, faith unifies us by shifting the focus from our own inadequacy onto God, and from him to the situation at hand. In believing in God, one is trusting in other resources than one's own. Ironically it is this trust that enables one to use one's *own* resources. The familiar dictum that "we have nothing to fear but fear itself" is true but not very helpful. Jesus warned against fear more than against anything else and often accompanied his warning with a reprimand for lack of faith: "Why are you afraid, O men of little faith?" (Matt. 8:26; see also Matt. 14:31; 17:17; Mark 4:40; Luke 24:25).

Fear can be a terrible bondage as it blocks us in our

efforts and deprives us of our "promised lands." Fear can, however, be overcome, providing we give its overcoming top priority. Realizing "we have nothing to fear but fear itself" is a move in this direction. By removing the focus from the object of our fear, something outside us, to fear itself, something inside us, we have identified the source of the problem. This is the first step. But problems are rarely overcome by identification alone, especially since the fear of something within us is usually more difficult to cope with than the fear of something outside ourselves. Determination is necessary too—but even determination can lack the wherewithal for overcoming. One needs also the capacity, the resources, for acting in spite of fear. Faith provides these resources. Trusting in the Power beyond our own dislodges our attention from its fixation to fear so that our imagination is freed to join with our faith in making the leap toward the positive. Faith provides the ability to direct ourselves in the midst of our fear. God did not give us a spirit of fear, but a spirit of power and love and self-direction (II Tim. 1:7).

Guilt

Another cause of double-mindedness is implicit in the fact that one of our minds is usually hidden. Our guilt over the unacceptability of this mind is a block to our receiving. I cannot receive what I desire, because I do not deserve it. I want—but I shouldn't have. Our self-image is not commensurate with our request.

This entrenchment of guilt is supported by some familiar pieties, purportedly Christian, in which to doubt one's self-worth is considered a laudable pursuit. In these pieties God is good in proportion to my being no good. Self-assertion is the equivalent of sinful pride, self-effacement the equivalent of humility, and self-disgust glories God.

Fortunately, sinful pride is much more complicated than self-assertion. In fact, self-effacement can be a form of pride. Self-disgust may actually be a disgust with God. Self-doubt is really a doubting of God. We do not believe he has the capacity to work through our own inadequacy. We are doubting his promises in the "faith of our Lord Jesus Christ" to do precisely this.

Painful areas in the self need to be faced so that they can be accepted and forgiven, not rejected. Fortunately we do not have to approve of all areas of our self before we can accept them—any more than our disapproval of them need lead us to reject them. For in rejecting any *part* of ourselves, we are in effect rejecting *ourselves*. By accepting our total self—the approved and disapproved—we are incorporating all areas of our self into our acceptance, and thereby taking the first step in overcoming our inner division. As we approach a degree of self-unification we are able to give direction to our efforts without being hampered by our double-mindedness. The unity created by acceptance makes possible the utilization of our energies, which are otherwise dissipated by inner division.

The love of God which is communicated in the faith of our Lord Jesus Christ offers us this unconditional acceptance. The love that Christ revealed is a love for our total self in which all our negativities are embraced by forgiveness. The guilt that divides us is overcome by reconciliation. We are thus encouraged to embrace ourselves in this same acceptance—to feel *good* about ourselves.

Friendship with the World

A third cause of double-mindedness is what James calls "friendship with the world," which he equates with "enmity with God." Here our double-mindedness is viewed as basically a conflict of loyalties. God and the world are placed in opposition, with opposing sets of priorities and values. Friendship with one excludes the other. The wisdom for which we ask in faith would put us at variance with the world, since the world's values and priorities are ultimately an unwise investment for our life's energies.

The values and priorities of the world appeal to our selfish desires. "You ask and do not receive, because you ask wrongly, to spend it on your passions." These passions are usually associated with pleasure, and for this reason pleasure is often identified with the world in its opposition to God. It may seem that James is only espousing a self-denying piety which has now fallen into disrepute. The contemporary emphasis is on self-assertion—on encouraging one another to say how we feel, on taking our own desires seriously. Each age seems to be attempting to correct the abuses created by the previous age. Consequently one might expect our age to be followed by a resurgence of self-denial as an antidote to the present self-seeking binge. It is to be hoped that this will not occur, since the swing from one extreme to another is obviously not progress, but only leads from one kind of double-mindedness to another.

The problem is not pleasure—even pleasure as an end

in itself. In identifying pleasure with worldliness, distorted pieties have made it difficult for those who espouse them to enjoy *anything* without feeling guilty, under the mistaken impression that enjoyment is at best irrelevant and frequently dangerous. These pieties place God in the unattractive role of a sadistic creator who makes pleasures available to his creatures and then makes them feel guilty if they enjoy them.

Friendship with the world is something other than seeking pleasures or gratification. Rather it is adopting a specific attitude toward such gratification. The values of the world permit a person to put gratification first, while other concerns, such as those associated with the needs of others, are given a lower priority.

Just as one form of friendship with the world is characterized by a pleasure priority, so another is characterized by self-aggrandizement in the accumulation of power. And as some people have denigrated pleasure in an attempt to solve such abuse, others also denigrate power as an entity in itself. Those influenced by such "solutions" to the problem may have grave misgivings when exercising power, as others experience guilt when involved in pleasure. They may even find a certain satisfaction in refusing to exercise power, just as people find satisfaction in denying themselves pleasure. The exercise of power, like the affirmation of pleasure, is a potentially healthy expression of life. So also are sensitivity to the needs of others, the refusal of immediate pleasure to obtain a later good, and the exercise of self-denial, even to the giving of one's life that another might live. These apparently contrasting qualities of life are not locked into either-or categories, though they are often presented as such. Rather they can and should reside in the same person. A person may, for example, seek to enjoy pleasure in one instance and in another to deny himself this satisfaction. What then governs his actions? The apparent answer is the situation at hand. As he perceives the context of any particular moment, he responds accordingly. But the response is not the instinctive response to the environment that we might anticipate in other forms of life. Rather one makes a decision, regardless of how habituated or conditioned one's actions may appear. What then influences the decision? One's sense of *who* or *whose* one is! If someone is a friend of God he has one identity; if he is a friend of the world he has another. If he is inclining in both directions, he is of a double mind.

Conflict of Loyalties

James calls those who have become friends of the world "unfaithful creatures." The literal translation is "adulteresses." The relationship between God and his people is like a marriage; and friendship with the world is like committing adultery.

Adultery is a traditional taboo largely because it undermines family stability. Since most societies are built on the family unit, adultery is perceived as undermining *societal* stability. A marital relationship is a responsible relationship with obligations, while an adulterous relationship is usually one with fewer obligations. Consequently adultery has traditionally been viewed as an irresponsible action in which loyalty is sacrificed for a more tangible satisfaction. The phrase "having an affair" indicates the rootlessness of most of these transactions. The clandestine nature usually associated with adultery has at least an initial appeal in the excitement of doing something naughty, which may linger on even among the sophisticated swingers.

Those having an "affair with the world" are likewise afflicted by the twinges of disloyalty. Their moments before God are uncomfortable because they are subliminally aware that they are playing games with him. The pleasures of the "affair" are a strong pull, but they are short-lived. Other satisfactions that one also values are undermined by the breach of commitment.

God also is not unaffected by the "affair." James describes him as a jealous lover: "He yearns jealously over the spirit which he has made to dwell in us." The conclusion to the Ten Commandments also describes God as a jealous God: "I the Lord your God am a jealous God" (Exod. 20:5). Though jealousy has a negative connotation in our day, this use of the word to describe God's response is meant to indicate how *much* he cares. Even in our day some marital partners interpret a lack of jealousy on the part of their mates as a lack of caring. We *belong* to God. He created us in his image. We function in harmony with our own natures when we are in a committed relationship with him. God is jealous of this relationship for *our* sake and is portrayed as one who remains faithful even when treated unfaithfully. The familiar symbol of love is the human heart. Like the faithfully pumping heart, love is constant, always reaching out, always available. "Love never ends"— never gives up.

Repentance as a Way of Removal

Obviously if we are to remove the obstacle of double-mindedness so that we can receive as well as ask, something has to change. James rises again to his prophetic function and calls for repentance: "Cleanse your hands, you sinners, and purify your hearts, you men of double mind." Respond to God's overture of love! To repent means to change one's mind—in this instance to move from a double mind to a unified mind—to rid ourselves of resistance to what supposedly we desire. If we are to achieve these desires, we will need to face all the resistance, hesitance, and double-mindedness that dissipate our quest.

Jesus described the determination of a unified mind by the parable of the merchant in search of fine pearls. When the merchant discovered a pearl of great price— analogous to the Kingdom of Heaven—he sold all that he had in order to buy it. He knew what he wanted and was willing to make the necessary sacrifices to have it.

In contrast, double-mindedness is prolonged indecision. The person is trapped by his own ambivalence; on the one hand he consciously desires to receive, and on the other he is resisting this very reception. Nor can he convincingly plead impotence. He can do something about his division. God makes overtures to us; he yearns jealously over the spirit which he has made to dwell in us; he calls us to the single-mindedness of faith. We are not victims of circumstances, but conspirators in these circumstances. Instead of making full use of the resources available to us, we play games with these resources.

"Resist the devil and he will flee from you," says James. With these words James describes the power inherent in simply making a decision. Once we "know our own mind" the adversary flees. We *can* say no. We can reject, cancel, dismiss the sabotaging impulse, the distracting sidetracks. If we talk ourselves into believing we are helpless before these divisive influences, we *will* be. On the other hand, if we assume, with James, that we have the resources to direct ourselves, we are likely to act as though we did. We may even surprise ourselves with what we can accomplish once we lift the self-imposed, or culturally imposed, limitations upon our potentials.

Deciding vs. Struggling

Our resources for directing ourselves involve more than resisting the negative: we can also direct ourselves toward the positive. "Draw near to God and he will draw near to you." From the context of these words it is evident that our drawing near to God is a response to his drawing near to us. Yet it seems to us when we make this move that we are taking the initiative. If, however, we conceive of our move as a response, our efforts gain added significance. We function then in the perspective of being guided—called—by God, and our response takes the shape of a commitment.

The power in a simple decision is the power of a single mind. We dissipate our energies in the perpetuation of a struggle between supposedly opposing forces at work within us. The struggle is actually an illusion of a struggle, since it is we ourselves who supply the energy to both of these forces. Consequently, the struggle is a smoke screen for our double-mindedness. We could cease the struggle if we willed ourselves to do so, since both of these minds belong to us. But to do so would mean that we no longer needed the evidence of a struggle to tolerate our perpetuation of double-mindedness. In other words, we would be ready to move—ready to decide. This decision, which is really a commitment, cuts through the duplicity of the struggle—and the struggle is over!

We *can* remove the obstacle of double-mindedness. It remains only because of what it symbolizes—our own duplicity. The resource for removing it is faith. We are creatures and not autonomous beings, and faith is an expression of our creatureliness. It is a response to the overture of God, who calls us to our own identity. As an act of commitment, faith is an integrating influence which transcends the double-mindedness and creates the openness to receive.

The causes of double-mindedness are difficult to eradicate. What is removed today can return tomorrow. Yet it is possible to learn to direct ourselves in spite of them. The sober alcoholic is still an alcoholic even though he is sober. So the anxious person may still be afflicted with fear even though he has the courage through his faith to act in the face of it. Feelings of guilt may continue to be a problem though we know the Good News of God's forgiveness. There may still be those times when we so disappoint ourselves that we reject ourselves in spite of the acceptance we have from God and his people— including those in our own family. Our desire then is to *think more highly* of ourselves—which our guilt prevents—rather than to accept ourselves. But we still have the potential of faith to respond to God's love and through his love also to love ourselves. Friendship with the world may be an on-and-off sort of affair. Because of the subtlety of the games we play, it is difficult at times to perceive when we are breaching our covenant with God and participating in a tryst with the world. As our wisdom increases, however, we catch on a little sooner. Cutting through the murkiness of self-deception, we can make the decision, without the fanfare of struggle, to reaffirm our identity by acknowledging again *whose* we are.

VI

Living Under the Law of Liberty

He who looks into the perfect law, the law of liberty, and perseveres, being no hearer that forgets but a doer that acts, he shall be blessed in his doing. (James 1:25)

My brethren, show no partiality as you hold the faith of our Lord Jesus Christ, the Lord of glory. (James 2:1)

If you really fulfil the royal law, according to the scripture, "You shall love your neighbor as yourself," you do well. But if you show partiality, you commit sin, and are convicted by the law as transgressors. For whoever keeps the whole law but fails in one point has become guilty of all of it. For he who said, "Do not commit adultery," said also, "Do not kill." If you do not commit adultery but do kill, you have become a transgressor of the law. So speak and so act as those who are to be judged under the law of liberty. For judgment is without mercy to one who has shown no mercy; yet mercy triumphs over judgment. (James 2:8-13)

The release from the bondage of double-mindedness, its causes and consequences, is described in the Bible by several metaphors. In depicting his mission of emancipation, Jesus, quoting the prophet Isaiah, said that he had come "to proclaim release to the captives . . . to set at liberty those who are oppressed." All this is "good news to the poor" (Luke 4:18). We cannot rule out physical incarceration and oppression as the bondage from which Jesus releases us, because the spirit of Christ is an influence for a more just and humane society. However, it is evident from other biblical sources and from subsequent history that the mission of Jesus may actually *lead* to incarceration and oppression for his followers. He himself was the victim of such oppression. But the Good News obviously is primarily concerned with the emancipation from the bondage of the mind— from the inhibiting powers of guilt, anxiety, bitterness, and depression. In our day we associate these negative forces with the low self-image which programs one to defeat and immobility. Paul describes this condition as "the spirit of slavery" in contrast to "the spirit of sonship" (Rom. 8:15). The release from this spirit of slavery comes through what James calls "the law of liberty."

Freedom Under the Perfect Law

"Law of liberty" may seem to be a contradiction in terms. How can law, any law, bring personal freedom? James shows an awareness of the problem by terming the law of liberty the "perfect" law and contrasting it with the familiar law of the commandments. This law of commandments has two traditional uses in the Christian tradition. The one is called the civil use, and refers to the orderly structure necessary for the functioning of society. The responsibility for the civil use is placed with the governments of society at both local and state levels.

The other is called "the law that accuses" and refers to the judgment of the individual conscience before God. It is this use that James describes in detail. The law of commandments convicts us all as we stand before God. Here, in truth, there is no discrimination, for we are all under judgment. "For whoever keeps the whole law but fails in one point has become guilty of all of it." Before God there are no levels of violation. The whole human race is pronounced guilty. "For he who said, 'Do not commit adultery,' said also, 'Do not kill.' If you do not commit adultery but do kill, you have become a transgressor of the law." This use of the law differs from the civil use where there are legitimate degrees of violation and, therefore, differences in penalties. There man is judging man. Before God there are no such gradations but rather a negatively oriented equality as a "fallen humanity."

After defining the law of commandments so precisely that no one can escape its judgment, James proclaims the Good News that we are no longer under the law that accuses but are under the law of liberty. Here the central issue is not judgment—rather it is mercy. "Mercy triumphs over judgment." The context of the law of liberty is radically different from that of the law that accuses; it is a context of grace. This difference in context accounts for the difference between those who hear the law but do not—or cannot—do it, and those who hear and do. In other words, the atmosphere of grace releases one from the bondage to guilt and its accompanying negative forces so that one is free to *do*.

Since we are no longer under God's judgment, no one is under ours either. We are released from a law-oriented judgment of people so that we can achieve new dimensions of appreciation. It is stultifying to the human spirit to be confined to a good-bad, right-wrong, success-failure type of evaluation. We miss so much of worth in ourselves and others when we cannot see beyond our limited categories of evaluation. In the milieu of grace we can receive ourselves and others as we and they are. This makes it possible for us to view people as entities in themselves, and not simply as they rate on a one- or two-dimensional scale. In fact, we can be free on occasion not to evaluate at all and to perceive people in their aesthetic wholeness where the adjective *beautiful* is applied to the person and not to tangible comparisons in appearance and function. Once we are liberated from the compulsion to evaluate, we can grow to know one another in the totality of our uniqueness.

Obviously we cannot apply this freedom from evaluation to the civil use of the law. The milieu of grace and the milieu of civil order constitute two distinguishable realms. Martin Luther called the realm of grace the realm of God's right hand, and the realm of societal order the realm of God's left hand. Though they are thus distinguished, these realms are not separated from each other, since God's people live in both realms and both realms are God's realms. In the realm of grace, however, God rules by the Good News of his unconditional love, and in the realm of societal order he rules by the law of commandments. In the former, the emphasis is on our fulfillment as persons, and in the latter the emphasis is on the insurance of safety, justice, and equality of opportunity in the social order. Here evaluations of all kinds in respect to persons need to be made for the achievement and maintenance of fair and workable social structures.

A Different Sort of Law

James uses the word *law* in "law of liberty" as John uses *commandment* in the commandment to love: "And this is his commandment, that we should believe in the name of his Son Jesus Christ and love one another, just as he has commanded us" (I John 3:23). Love, like liberty, is hardly something that can be legislated or commanded. The word is used in these instances in a broad sense meaning "proclamation" or "principle of operation."

James terms the commandment "You shall love your neighbor as yourself" the royal law. The opposite of this royal law is showing partiality. We cannot discriminate among neighbors: all are to be loved as ourselves. The prime example of showing partiality, for James, is the way society discriminates against the poor.

Functioning through mercy which triumphs over judgment, the law of liberty is reciprocal in nature: those who receive mercy also give it, and those who give it also receive it. Likewise, "judgment is without mercy to one who has shown no mercy." This principle of reciprocity is familiarly stated in the Lord's Prayer: "Forgive us our trespasses as we forgive those who trespass against us." There can be no partiality in such reciprocity.

This mutuality in the bestowal of mercy is initiated by the mercy bestowed by God which undergirds the law of liberty. It is basically *his* mercy which triumphs over *his* judgment. In the devotional tradition of the Greek Orthodox Church, there is a contemplative prayer which one of the fathers of this tradition said could teach one everything—the Jesus prayer: "Lord Jesus Christ, have mercy upon me." While our Western mind might consider this prayer too inadequate to merit much contemplation, it is basically a concentration on receiving. Meditating upon it is an antidote to the spirit of arrogance in which judgment triumphs over mercy. People who are arrogant usually manifest little awareness of having received *anything* of worth from another, let alone mercy.

The fact that we receive mercy is a reminder of our complicity in the problem of evil. Such a reminder may prevent us from casting stones at a fellow offender, since we ourselves are not without sin. The mercy bestowed in the law of liberty is nondiscriminatory like the judgment reckoned by the law of commandments. It can be given *by* all because it has been given *to* all, for God shows no partiality.

The importance of impartiality is applicable also to the civil use of the law. Justice is not for some but for all. Neither race nor creed nor class should determine who receives the opportunities in the social order. When a society becomes partial in its concern for justice, it comes under the judgment of God. To make this judgment known God calls forth the prophet to speak for him. It was in this manner that the prophets of Israel whom James admires were pressed into service—and likewise James in his own prophetic ministry.

There is good reason to consider the structures and

institutions of society as entities in themselves and not simply as aggregates of people. William Stringfellow sees the biblical witness to this autonomy of social structures in the term "principalities and powers" and the treatment of these as creatures: "Human beings are reluctant to acknowledge institutions—or any other principalities—as creatures having their own existence, personality and mode of life. Yet the Bible consistently speaks of the principalities as creatures" *(An Ethic for Christians and Other Aliens in a Strange Land* [Waco, Texas: Word Books, 1973], p. 79). As autonomous entities in a fallen world, these corporate structures and institutions with their values and priorities are fallen creatures. They are not simply subject to corruption because they are composed of corruptible people, but as entities in themselves are also *sources* of corruption. As Stringfellow puts it, "Corporations and nations and other demonic powers restrict, control, and consume human life in order to sustain and extend and prosper their own survival" (p. 84).

We show a common awareness of this corrupting influence of social organizations when we refer to persons as "organization men," or as having "become institutionalized," or as having been "corrupted by the system," and to institutions as being "dehumanizing" and "depersonalizing." Not only do persons influence institutions, but institutions influence persons. By the same token, injustice can become institutionalized so that those influenced by such institutions may be unaware of their discriminating characteristics. We take "the system" for granted—become familiarized with it—until somebody like a prophet brings its discrepancies to our attention. Then we either accept the judgment or defend the system. In the latter instance we usually also attack the prophet. Because social organizations are entities in themselves, racism, for example, has become institutionalized in our own society along with similar discriminations against the poor in general and minority groups in particular. Prophets have arisen to protest these discriminations, but as Jesus pointed out, "no prophet is acceptable in his own country," and, we might add, in his own time.

The Threatening Mirror

Though societal institutions are entities in themselves in a fallen world and are the objects of divine judgment, they are not the objects of divine mercy. It is *persons* who are forgiven by God, and consequently it is *persons* who can function under the law of liberty. But not all who are offered mercy accept it. Some continue to remain under judgment and simply suffer. Others attempt to justify themselves: in one way or another they try to convince themselves and others that they are justified by their own rightness.

We are usually best at this sort of self-justification when we are quarreling. As we lose awareness of a need for mercy, we document the case for our own innocence with much verbal punctuation, and not only fail to convince others but also fail to convince ourselves. Stressing our virtues as a cover for our failures, minimizing our transgressions in comparison to those of others, and pointing to others who are equally culpable to minimize the gravity of our own transgressions, are not ways by which we become free. The law that accuses is no less relentless when the guilt is corporate, nor is its judgment mitigated by our attempts to minimize our offenses. In fact, these attempts to defend ourselves only further entrench us in the spirit of slavery.

The mirror is always a threat when we elect to justify ourselves. As James points out, when we look into the mirror the tendency is to forget the image that we saw: "He observes himself and goes away and at once forgets what he was like" (1:24). We have heard much in recent years about the nature of such "forgetting." Freud called it repression. When what we see in the mirror is threatening to the security system by which we hold ourselves together, we have the capacity to block out the threatening image in order to survive. We lose our awareness of what we saw by avoiding it, evading it, and ultimately denying it.

Yet the process is not foolproof: we cannot completely forget. The twinge of the threatening memory of the mirror image is still with us,—but subliminally, so that we are more aware of the anxiety produced by the image than of the image itself. The spirit of fear is still present to obstruct our functioning. The mirror, of course, is available, but the tendency is not to look very closely when our sense of self-esteem is at stake. We fashion our protective blinders and give the mirror only a cursory glance. The law that accuses is too much for us. It provides more self-knowledge than we can bear; the reflection in the mirror is too uncomfortable to tolerate.

Under the law of liberty there is no need for forgetting, repressing, and running from reality, since there is no judgment—for mercy has triumphed over it.

The threat of the mirror is considerably reduced when one is forgiven. The receiving of mercy makes forgetting unnecessary. Yet old habits are hard to break, and resistance to freedom may linger on. The emotional repercussions of our hang-ups develop a momentum of their own and persist even when the basis for the hang-up is removed. Also the potential for self-rejection and denial is still with us even when we are under the law of liberty, and new tensions may revive these old patterns and tapes. The law of liberty provides the capability for working through the resistance of these emotionally enforced habit patterns. We need to initiate ways of coping and responding in situations which heretofore have stimulated only destructive patterns. By repeating these new ways we develop new habit patterns to replace the old.

Our Response to Guilt

The process of liberation begins with the critical question of how we respond to our guilt. The fact that we are under the law of liberty rather than the law of commandments does not mean that we no longer experience guilt. The differnce lies in what we do with it once we have it. Guilt is an uncomfortable tension in our psyches that informs us that we are not what we feel we should or ought to be. Sometimes it is specific—relating to "sins of commission or omission." Sometimes it relates solely to the nature of our fantasies and feelings. Once we become aware of this tension of guilt, how do we respond to it? Do we use it to berate ourselves? Do we mentally punish ourselves by becoming depressed, judging ourselves as worthless, or feeling badly about ourselves? These are unfortunately rather common ways of responding to guilt—ways to which the law of liberty would put an end.

If there were any value in these ways of responding to guilt, the misery they bring upon us might be tolerated. But actually they have only a negative effect on us. Imagine treating another person, particularly a child, in the same way. Visualize yourself berating a child for his shortcomings the way you berate yourself. What would it accomplish? Would the child be motivated and inspired to do better? More than likely he would feel beaten down and defeated, full of hate for himself and for you, and less able than before to believe in his own worth and to take hold and do. This is precisely the effect this approach has when applied to ourselves—to the Child within us. We are obviously going to have to cease this kind of Parental approach toward ourselves if we hope to effect any change in our living. The mercy of God provides us with the freedom to do precisely this. We can become merciful and kind toward ourselves rather than continuing to be unmerciful and cruel.

Because of the destructive way in which so many of us respond to our guilt, guilt itself is sometimes treated as an evil. We talk then as though we would like to eliminate guilt. Fortunately this cannot be done— although some people make a desperate effort to do so. Even if it could be done, we would be eliminating something basic to our humanity. Guilt is not our enemy; rather it is our friend. Our response to it, however, *is* our enemy.

The negative response to guilt is conditioned by

judgment based on the law that accuses. Under the law of liberty, judgment is removed, and therefore the negative response should cease. Instead one can face guilt positively and constructively. This does not mean that we automatically will, but we have the potential to work at it. Nor does it mean that we will not continue to feel badly about our failures. If others are hurt or otherwise disturbed by our behavior, we feel it deeply because these others are often persons we care about. We feel the pain we believe we have inflicted on them. Even this kind of sorrow, however, can be corrupted by our egotism, which tends to exaggerate the amount of influence we have on others.

Some of this sorrow may be simply our hurt pride. We had hoped to think better of ourselves—and perhaps had been doing so for a period of time—but now that we have erred, goofed, sinned, we cannot. So we are disgusted and angry with ourselves. In the heat of this self-disgust we may withdraw from the overtures of others— particularly the overture of reconciliation. We want instead to be alone in our misery to preoccupy ourselves with our defeat. It is to be hoped we soon see the stupidity of any prolongation of such sorrowing, swallow our pride, learn once again what it means to accept ourselves as we are, and return to the human fellowship with a new sense of humility.

Some of this sorrow over our failures may also be a submissive sorrow. Our obligation is not just to ourselves, but to God. So in our guilt we "humble ourselves before the Lord." Our defenses are down and we are open for acceptance. This is the sorrow of repentance—

when we "mourn" and even "weep" in the presence of God.

Jesus illustrated this sorrow by the story of the two men who went into the temple to pray, one a Pharisee and the other a tax collector (Luke 18:9-14). Although the Pharisee was praying, his prayer was directed more to his own ego than to God; it is an example of seeking to avoid judgment by self-justification: "God, I thank thee that I am not like other men, extortioners, unjust, adulterers, or even like this tax collector." He believed in a gradation of sins and saw himself at a much lower grade than those who were notoriously sinful. He also had some compensating virtues: "I fast twice a week, I give tithes of all that I get."

In contrast, the tax collector would not even lift his eyes to heaven. As the Pharisee indicated, he probably had reason for feeling judged: his profession was synonymous with graft and corruption and betrayal. Yet he was in sorrow for his unsavory ways. He "beat his breast, saying, 'God, be merciful to me a sinner!'" Then Jesus made his point: "I tell you, this man went down to his house justified rather than the other." Why? Because *God* had justified him. "For every one who exalts himself will be humbled, but he who humbles himself will be exalted." James' words are almost identical: "Humble yourselves before the Lord and he will exalt you" (4:10).

To be exalted means literally to be raised up— elevated. The sorrow of repentance is resolved by reconciliation. The humbled spirit is resurrected. He is inspired—secure in his own identity, knowing *whose* he is. Mercy has triumphed over judgment. He is integrated for action—ready for change. The law of liberty has freed him from the bondage of guilt. The tension remains, but its judgment has been removed. For the elevated spirit, the tension of guilt is an asset in effecting change. He can use this guilt as helpful feedback in learning from experience. The tension created by the gap between where we are and where we would like to be is in itself a potential source of self-improvement and growth. When the sting of defeat has been resolved we can mentally relive the incident of failure, noting the various factors that contributed to it. We achieve insight into the kind of games that we were playing and into the double-mindedness that was involved. Then we can mentally relive the incident the way we would like to have functioned, exercising our freedom to do it differently in our minds.

When we use our guilt for reflective feedback on our behavior, and follow through with mental reruns and trial runs, we are better prepared for the next opportunity to do things differently. Since our guilt is no longer a destructive tension for self-beratement but rather a positive tension for self-improvement, our bondage to defeat is over. It is thus that the law of liberty becomes a means for change—for doing things differently and doing them better. Through it we are liberated to mobilize our resources for our own growth.

The Fear of Freedom

Freedom is frightening. It leads we know not where. We know the boundaries of our bondage. Although we hate them and chafe under them, they provide a security of sorts—what Karen Horney calls "the security of the familiar." In contrast, the vistas of freedom, regardless of how positively we may anticipate them, are lacking in boundaries. They contain the elements of the unknown or unexperienced. The escape from such freedom is a well-documented human perversion. I have wanted to run from it, and perhaps you have also. We may find it actually comforting at times to talk ourselves out of freedom. We are more content with our bondage then, or at least feel less guilty about remaining within its boundaries. Our challenge is to give up the paltry security that is based primarily on familiar landmarks, for a more genuine security based on the experience of growth.

The law of liberty with its basis in the mercy of God makes it possible for us to enter more and more into the new—the new creation in Christ Jesus, whose we are. Although we slip back into our old and self-defeating ways, we can use these experiences, badly as they make us feel, to provide us with added understanding of ourselves and others. Our failures can also help to further stabilize us in the freedom which is ours through the mercy of God.

VII

Power to Do—to Act—Now— Differently

Be doers of the word, and not hearers only, deceiving yourselves. For if any one is a hearer of the word and not a doer, he is like a man who observes his natural face in a mirror; for he observes himself and goes away and at once forgets what he was like. (James 1:22-24)

Some one will say, "You have faith and I have works." Show me your faith apart from your works, and I by my works will show you my faith. You believe that God is one; you do well. Even the demons believe—and shudder. Do you want to be shown, you shallow man, that faith apart from works is barren? Was not Abraham our father justified by works, when he offered his son Isaac upon the altar? You see that faith was active along with his works, and faith was completed by works, and the scripture was fulfilled which says, "Abraham believed God, and it was reckoned to him as righteousness"; and he was called the friend of God. You see that a man is justified by works and not by faith alone. And in the same way was not also Rahab the harlot justified by works when she received the messengers and sent them out another way? For as the body apart from the spirit is dead, so faith apart from works is dead. (James 2:18-26)

Whoever knows what is right to do and fails to do it, for him it is sin. (James 4:17)

Freedom is one thing, and power to utilize the freedom positively is another. We sometimes use these words, *freedom* and *power*, interchangeably, for power implies freedom. The converse, however, is not so; freedom does not imply power. Freedom means release from the obstacles and hindrances which prevent us from doing what we desire. Power, on the other hand, means having the capacity to do what we desire, once we obtain the freedom. Contrary to what those in bondage usually assume, becoming free is not the same as being able to do. Although we cannot achieve our desires without becoming free to pursue them, we need something beyond freedom—namely, power—to achieve them.

Faith as Power

In the final interview televised before his death former President Lyndon Johnson gave a political illustration of the relationship between freedom and power. Reflecting upon his civil rights activities in the middle sixties, he stated that he and his advisors discovered that simply achieving civil rights legislation which guaranteed minority persons specific freedoms that previously had been denied them did not necessarily mean that these persons could assume the citizenship responsibilities involved in these freedoms. They had reasoned that if the door was opened, the minority persons would obviously walk through it. Instead they discovered that people who had been denied their liberties for long periods of time needed help to walk through the newly opened doors. Politically this help consisted in providing educational and vocational opportunities for these persons so that they would develop the ability to use their freedom as responsible citizens.

For James, the law of liberty not only makes one free; one is also able to act in one's freedom: "He who looks into the perfect law, the law of liberty, and perseveres, being no hearer that forgets but a doer that acts, he shall be blessed in his doing" (1:25). The power for doing under the law of liberty is the power of *faith*. Faith, for James, is an openness to receive what God wants to give us and, consequently, a power for doing. It leads to works, which in the context of the letter means works of mercy, compassion, and caring. Faith is "completed by works," that is, its meaning is fulfilled in our lives when we extend to others the compassion which we have received from God.

This understanding of faith is basic to the differentiation between a hearer who forgets and a doer who acts. Faith is not simply belief—not even belief in the existence of God. One can acknowledge God's existence in a negative way and "shudder." Nor is faith simply believing certain things *about* God. As an example, James cites the Old Testament emphasis on monotheism in contrast to the polytheism of neighboring peoples: "You believe that God is one; you do well. Even the demons believe—and shudder."

To understand what faith is, we must go beyond faith's cognitive content—its beliefs—to its dynamic character. Faith is believing *in* God, and consequently contains the attitude of trust. There is a difference between believing as trust and believing as recognizing what one considers to be a fact. On the basis of sense perception, for example, we may believe that which we see is factual.

Some people believe that they have factual evidence for life after death; yet even the religious nature of this supposed reality does not make their acceptance of it a faith. Faith goes with faithfulness, whereas accommodating oneself to the facts goes with adaptation for survival. This is the essential truth of Jesus' story of the rich man and Lazarus (Luke 16:19-31).

Lazarus was so poor that he ate the scraps from the rich man's table as a beggar. After their deaths, however, their positions were reversed, for Lazarus was in heaven and the rich man in hell. Calling across the abyss that he could not cross, the rich man asked the patriarch Abraham to send Lazarus back from the dead to warn his brothers, who were living in the same way he had, lest they too end up in hell; for he reasoned, "If some one goes to them from the dead, they will repent."

But Abraham was not impressed by the argument: "If they do not hear Moses and the prophets, neither will they be convinced if some one should rise from the dead." They would not be convinced in the sense of being changed—of being converted from their suspicious and arrogant ways to the way of trust and compassion. They might make some patchwork adaptations, but they would still be essentially their same old selves. They already had the opportunity for the kind of conviction the rich man desired for them—the Old Covenant of Moses and the prophets, to which they could respond in *faith* and *repent*.

Faith in this context is faith in *God*. It is relationship-centered rather than belief-centered. Beliefs are present in faith, but always in the context of a relationship with the Object of faith. The knowledge that is associated with faith—what we believe about God and how he relates to his people—has its context in the process of *knowing* God, or, as James would put it, of being friends of God.

From Defeat to Victory

James assumes that through our faith we have the power to act, and that we are deceiving ourselves if we do not acknowledge this power. We cannot plead helplessness, for this is simply an avoidance of the responsibility that goes with being faithful. It is a return to the divided allegiances of double-mindedness. "Whoever knows what is right to do and fails to do it, for him it is sin."

There are many substitutes for action by which we deceive ourselves. We have already discussed rhetoric as one of these, in which high-sounding words are used to conceal the fact that nothing much will come of them. Illness is another potential substitute for action. How often the plea "I don't feel good" gets us off the responsibility hook. Most of us at one time or another have probably exploited this easy out, but there are others whose illnesses have become chronic excuses for avoiding responsible action.

Ironically the means for overcoming illness can also be used as a substitute for responsible action. It has been documented that people tend to feel better after visiting a physician regardless of what treatment he offers. Going to the doctor, therefore, can become an end in itself rather than a means for healing. The same can happen in counseling and psychotherapy. So long as someone is seeing a physician or a counselor, he is ostensibly doing something about his emotional or physical problems. In actuality, however, he may be continuing his resistance to responsible action, using the fact that he is "under doctor's care," or "undergoing psychotherapy," as an additional excuse. It is no mystery, then, why he may become dependent upon counseling or "doctoring" and seek to prolong it.

The most common substitute for action is waiting for the ideal conditions before we act. Those who use this way of escape project their responsibilities onto others—including God. They have many reasons why they cannot act *now*, all involving circumstances beyond their control. Others have to change—the world has to change—before they can change. Until then they continue to be victimized by circumstances that render them helpless. Gestalt therapist Fritz Perls is thoroughly "Jamesian" when he says that "I can't equals I won't." But the double mind is hidden and "I can't" is often uncontested.

The power of a relationship is in the confidence and security it stimulates. We can receive this kind of support from our relationships with friends and family. So also with the relationship of faith. God's Spirit, says Paul, bears witness with our spirit that we are the children of God. Paul Tournier calls the relationship of faith the "inner dialogue." This dialogue is not a substitute for external dialogues with others, any more than God is a substitute for people. God is known through his people and not apart from them. His Word is given to a fellowship of believers—the church—and not to isolated believers. Yet we can know the inner dialogue when we are in solitude. In this sense we are never really alone. The confidence that comes through this spiritual relationship was expressed ebulliently by Paul when he said, "I can do all things through him who strengthens me" (Phil. 4:13).

This same Paul has also given us what is perhaps our most familiar expression of moral impotence: "I do not understand my own actions. For I do not do what I want, but I do the very thing I hate. . . . I do not do the good I want, but the evil I do not want is what I do" (Rom. 7:15, 19). Here is the frustration of defeat—the anguish not only of helplessness but of perverseness. We can easily identify with it. We know the ruts we get into: the tapes we play in our heads that relentlessly overwhelm our resistance, the scripts we follow as though predestined, the habits we hate but nevertheless repeat. We know how these perverse forces within us bog us down in defeat, frustrate our growth, and lead us to the suffering of futility. It is to be hoped we are too honest to engage in the tricks of denial, the ingenuity of rationalization and other defenses, to protect us from the truth. So we suffer instead.

Because we identify so clearly with Paul's lament, it is often quoted as though it were the culmination of the gospel. As such it is inadvertently used to program us to defeat. The context in which Paul voiced his frustration, however, is one of hope and not despair. His defeat is not the end of his faith, but rather the prelude to victory. The agony of defeat reaches its climax with the cry "Wretched man that I am! Who will deliver me from this body of death?" This is more a gut expression of "bottoming out" than a question. Paul knows the answer:

"Thanks be to God through Jesus Christ our Lord" (Rom. 7:24, 25).

From this point on, the lament is over, and Paul describes instead the exaltation that follows the bottoming out—the victory that follows the defeat: "There is therefore now no condemnation for those who are in Christ Jesus. . . . In all these things we are more than conquerors through him who loved us. For I am sure that neither death, nor life, . . . nor anything else in all creation, will be able to separate us from the love of God in Christ Jesus our Lord" (Rom. 8:1, 37-39). This is the gospel, the Good News, the faith of our Lord Jesus Christ, the law of liberty. We experience judgment upon ourselves; we accept the judgment, suffering its pain; we ask for mercy, and by faith we receive it. The doors of our prison swing open. We are not only reconciled but exalted. Inspired with confidence, we can act—do things differently, turn off the tapes, change the script, direct ourselves, enter the *new*.

The Acceptance of Powerlessness

It is ironical that the pursuit of power to effect change should end in the acceptance of powerlessness. Paul's dynamic expression of this paradox is probably what attracted Martin Luther to him rather than to James. Luther too had cried out in the agony of defeat, "Wretched man that I am! Who will deliver me?" The power for change centers in the acceptance of the self unchanged. As Sören Kierkegaard put it, if we are going to move *from* the spot, we must begin *at* the spot: "To become is a movement from the spot, but to become oneself is a movement at the spot." We may not like reality, but if we are going to change it we first have to accept it. The initial step in the recovery program of Alcoholics Anonymous is "We admit we are powerless over alcohol, that our lives have become unmanageable." What is true of alcohol applies also to whatever has us in bondage, leads us to feel trapped, bound, and programmed to defeat.

In spite of the clarity of the Christian tradition and addiction therapies' documentation of the fact that the way to power is through the acceptance of powerlessness, we still try to work around it. We find it hard on our pride to admit our defeats, and so we try instead to convince ourselves that we really could be victorious if we wanted to. So long as we are not forced to test this assumption, the illusion of power may suffice to hold us together.

Our cultural values support such illusions. The work ethic which undergirds our economy is based on the assumption that we can accomplish just about anything by hard work. Consequently, if we worked at it, we could do it! The other cultural assumption is that change comes through willpower: if a person really *wants* to do something, he will do it. There is no room in such assumptions for the ineffectiveness of work or the impotency of the will.

While these cultural norms have served to make us the nation that excels in the area of technology, they have not been as successful in the fulfillment of our persons. Working with *things* can detract from our personal development as well as contribute to it. Willpower when applied to ourselves runs into the formidable obstacle of a divided will. The end of such doubleness comes not through willpower but through reconciliation. The will that emerges from our unification is not the old and divided will which programmed us to defeat but a new and united will which is empowered by faith. The old is still present to harass the new, but the inner relationship of the Spirit is a dynamic support for continuous *re*newal.

My initial attraction to James following our family tragedy centered in his affirmation of power. He does not describe the exaltation process in a dynamic way as does Paul. Rather he simply assumes it and, on the basis of it, opens the imagination to new horizons for living. In the shock of bereavement one is overwhelmed by one's helplessness and powerlessness, a passive though agonized victim of a capricious and cruel world. One needs to have one's balance restored, and James helped me to do this. His affirmation of the power of faith to effect change was the light I needed to penetrate an otherwise dark and painful existence. Paul's description of moral impotence did not match my primary awareness, which was rather of a total impotence before the capricious forces of life. We are painfully limited by forces beyond our control, and consequently are pathetically vulnerable to the tragic dimensions of life. At the same time we also have the resources to utilize the freedom that we have in a creative and responsible way.

Faith and the Imagination

Faith catches—and captures—the imagination. In fact, the two are closely related. Faith stimulates the visualization of the promises of God—what he can do with our lives. It challenges us on the basis of the commitment of our inner dialogue to believe that what we have envisioned of his promises shall be so—to say *amen* to it. This is programming for the positive—for victory—and is the opposite of the programming for defeat of the double mind. Our actions may then follow the tracks laid in our imagination by faith. As Thoreau put it in *Walden,* "If one advances confidently in the direction of his dreams and endeavors to live the life which he has imagined, he will meet with success unimagined in common hours."

The power we receive through faith is the power to change ourselves—not others. This may be disappointing to us, since we are often convinced that if only we could change others—our children, mates, parents, friends—our own problems would be over. We are prone, as Jesus said, to focus on the specks in our neighbor's eye, even suggesting that he allow us to take them out, while at the same time not even noticing the logs that are in our own eyes. Yet it is precisely our own logs that are blocking our growth. Nothing will change this until we face up to their presence. While this is a painful step and one which we would like to avoid, it is also a necessary step toward becoming reconciled with our total persons. The power to accept, to receive, forgiveness for the logs in our own eyes, is the power to overcome them—to remove them.

In Abraham Maslow's hierarchy of human needs, self-actualization is at the top. While some have criticized the concept of self-actualization as being self-centered rather than socially oriented, as Maslow defines it self-actualization, like Jung's concept of individuation, takes place in the milieu of interpersonal relationships. We develop our full potential as persons—which for

Maslow includes spiritual potential—only as we participate in receiving and giving within the human community.

Even though spiritually oriented, self-actualization as Maslow conceives it is still in need of a Christian context for our purposes. We actualize our potentials under God through the same grace which has provided them. Actualizing our potentials under God means growing into the likeness of God as this has been revealed in Jesus Christ. This likeness or image of God is not only our destiny, but also our origin. Though we are "fallen" from this likeness, it is still our basic identity. Through the reconciliation with our fallenness which God offers us through Christ, we receive the power of faith to do things differently, rather than to follow the same old patterns, ruts, and habits associated with our fallenness. We have received the power to move from the spot by beginning at the spot. Forgiveness grounds us in a positive realism at the spot—where we are—and thereby makes available to us the faith to move, to overcome, to change, to grow, to actualize our identity as sons and daughters of God.

While the power we receive to effect change applies to changing ourselves and not others, changes in ourselves do affect others. By the same token changes in others affect us. As we have seen, the works that faith brings about are works of compassion and mercy. We need the support and care of others. We are more readily aware of how much we are indebted to others when we have received the care and compassion we needed in times of crisis. Yet we are often unaware of how much we are receiving constantly from significant others and groups in our lives in non-crisis times. Obviously we are influenced—yes, changed—by our relationship with these people. Yet the change is not something that is done for us, but rather something that we do through the resources of faith and confidence that relationships provide. Faith, after all, is a relationship-oriented power, and the inner dialogue through which it functions is supported by external dialogues with caring people. Those who receive and those who give are equally blessed in a caring community.

VIII
Taming the Tongue

*Know this, my beloved brethren. Let every man be quick to
hear, slow to speak, slow to anger, for the anger of man does
not work the righteousness of God. (James 1:19-20)*

*Above all, my brethren, do not swear, either by heaven or by
earth or with any other oath, but let your yes be yes and your no
be no, that you may not fall under condemnation. (James 5:12)*

*We all make many mistakes, and if any one makes no
mistakes in what he says he is a perfect man, able to bridle the
whole body also. If we put bits into the mouths of horses that
they may obey us, we guide their whole bodies. Look at the
ships also; though they are so great and are driven by strong
winds, they are guided by a very small rudder wherever the will
of the pilot directs. So the tongue is a little member and boasts
of great things. How great a forest is set ablaze by a small fire!
   And the tongue is a fire. The tongue is an unrighteous world
among our members, staining the whole body, setting on fire
the cycle of nature, and set on fire by hell. For every kind of
beast and bird, of reptile and sea creature, can be tamed and
has been tamed by humankind, but no human being can tame
the tongue–a restless evil, full of deadly poison. With it we bless
the Lord and Father, and with it we curse men, who are made
in the likeness of God. From the same mouth come blessing and*

121

*cursing. My brethren, this ought not to be so. Does a spring
pour forth from the same opening fresh water and brackish?
Can a fig tree, my brethren, yield olives, or a grapevine figs?
No more can salt water yield fresh. (James 3:2-12)*

It is one thing to affirm the power to effect change in
our lives—to do things differently; it is another to spell
out where and how this change takes place. While James
may be short on theological theory and on describing
psychological dynamics, he is long on the practical
applications of theory and on pinpointing behavioral
change. For James, the power to effect change in our
lives focuses on communication—specifically the use of
the tongue: "If any one thinks he is religious, and does
not bridle his tongue but deceives his heart, this man's
religion is vain" (1:26). As James' definition of religion
was clearly a definition of its application to human
relationships, so this definition of its failure is also in this
area. The choice of speech as the focus for behavioral
change goes to the heart of human relationships.

A Symbol of Evil

In spite of our growing understanding of the communication abilities of some of the higher animals, the power
of speech still distinguishes human beings from other
forms of life. Ironically most of our figures of speech
about speech are negative: "Mind your tongue," "Keep
your mouth shut," "Button your lip," "Shut up," and,
with the advent of Archie Bunker, "Stifle yourself." We
even refer to its negative use as a disease, namely,

foot-in-mouth disease. We know when we have it, because we wish we could take something back we have already said—and cannot. The irony of the aphorism "Silence is golden" corresponds to Job's "counsel" to his three windy friends: "Oh that you would keep silent, / and it would be your wisdom" (Job 13:5).

There are also proverbs and metaphors expressing the positive aspects of speech. "A word fitly spoken/is like apples of gold in a setting of silver" (Prov. 25:11). We admire those who "know just what to say," and respect others who "wax eloquent" in this or that cause.

James' description of this mixed blessing is definitely weighted toward the negative. The harsh things he says about the tongue stem from his use of this organ as a symbol of evil. In so doing he is following a familiar biblical pattern of employing organs of the body to symbolize personal attributes. The heart is used as a symbol of love, the abdomen or "bowels" as a symbol of compassion and affection. James' use of the tongue, however, is singular in its negative symbolism.

The perverseness of the tongue is demonstrated by the fact that, although its purpose is to reveal, we use it instead to deceive—even ourselves—and to berate others, using the terms *tongue-lash, put-down, gossip,* and *slander* as labels for such aggression. James' description is even more vivid: "How great a forest is set ablaze by a small fire! And the tongue is a fire. The tongue is an unrighteous world among our members, staining the whole body, setting on fire the cycle of nature, and set on fire by hell." James obviously sees the tongue as disrupting the rhythm, the harmonious function, of life in community.

What the tongue needs is a bridle, a rudder, a guide. Unbridled it is subject to impulse rather than direction. The negative consequences of speaking on impulse are reflected in the expression "He talks and then thinks." Unfortunately we tend to confuse acting on impulse with spontaneity. On the surface they often look alike, but actually they are quite different, for whereas spontaneous behavior is open, honest, and congruent, acting on impulse is a sign of inner division. It is as though our inner Child saw an opportunity to act first while the internalized Parent was looking elsewhere. When we act on impulse, we get the jump on our conscience. When the conscience finally begins to function, we have had the time to develop a good rationalization for the behavior. While spontaneity is the expression of the unified mind, impulsive behavior is an expression of the double mind, as the unaccepted self gets in a fast job—a quick end run. The bridle for an impulsive tongue, therefore, is a unified mind.

The tongue is not only the symbol of communication, but, for James, the symbol of the failure of communication. Marital problems are probably the most familiar example of the way in which communication failure stimulates strife. The purpose of marriage counseling is to facilitate communication, not between strangers but between intimates. Supposedly they know each other well, and yet they may not be able to communicate in any genuine way. In my own experience in marriage counseling, I have been impressed by the fact that two who sit beside each other each tell *me* how they feel about the other, rather than telling the other. My response is, "Tell her (him)—she's (he's) sitting right there." It seems amazingly difficult for either husband or wife actually to turn and look at the spouse.

When they do speak directly to each other, sparks may begin to fly. When this happens, I at times interrrupt the heated exchange by saying, "Before you answer her (him), tell me what she (he) said." Most of the time neither husband nor wife is able to do this to the other's satisfaction. "That's not what I said!" "Then what did you say?" After the mate repeats his or her statement, the other tries again to restate it. This time he or she usually succeeds. By then much of the heat has been dissipated—since many of our irritations are based on misunderstandings and preconceived ideas.

The failure to use words in communication accounts for much of this misunderstanding. Bill is a case in point in his marriage to Gloria. Gloria's complaint was that Bill never showed her any appreciation. Bill protested, "That's not true!" I asked him to elaborate. "I may not use pretty words like her dad does with her mother, but I still show it," he replied. Gloria challenged him to give an example. "Just yesterday," he said, "I came home for lunch when I could have stayed in town."

"That's appreciation?" Gloria retorted. "All that meant was I had to fix something extra for lunch."

"See what I mean?" Bill said, looking defeatedly at me. "She doesn't understand."

When I asked him to explain, he said, "I came home because I wanted to be with her—because I—I appreciate her."

"Well, why didn't you say that?" Gloria asked.

"Why should I have to say it?" Bill asked. "I was *doing* it."

Bill needed to learn that while actions speak louder than words, they also need to be accompanied by words: otherwise they may fail to "speak" at all. Our actions need *labels*. As the prophet Hosea counseled the people of Israel in their spiritual apostasy, "Take with you words/and return to the Lord" (Hos. 14:2).

Our communication with God—a relationship which the Bible compares to a marriage—is through Word and sacraments. Both are needed for fulfilling communication. Sacraments are rites in which communication is dramatized by symbolic actions. Yet in the sacraments such as baptism and the Lord's Supper, words are used to label the actions. Bill's action in coming home for lunch was like a sacrament—but it lacked the accompanying words. When joined with words, however, it could be a very effective way of revealing to Gloria his appreciation of her.

A Bridled Tongue

James offers a structure by which the tongue can be bridled: "Know this, my beloved brethren. Let every man be quick to hear, slow to speak, slow to anger." One who is quick to hear is a good listener. Those who live closely with blind persons comment that they do not have to repeat what they say to the blind, as they often do with those who can see. Perhaps this is due to an increased development of the sense of hearing in compensation for the deficiency in sight. It may also be due to the fact that sight may interfere with hearing. Not only is sight distracting to hearing, it is also at times threatening. In addition to the tone of voice, the nonverbal communication which the eye alone perceives can be so disconcerting that one fails to concentrate on the actual words being spoken. Consequently it takes courage to listen, particularly to what we do not want to hear, and to respond with words appropriate to our listening.

When we are quick to listen and slow to speak, we give others a chance to be heard. Many people have difficulty finding someone who will really listen to them. One who listens to such a person will "draw him out" so that he expresses himself, which in turn helps him to feel better about himself—and the world. To help meet this need many communities have trained volunteers who conduct a telephone service for troubled persons who want someone to talk to.

The tone in which words are spoken is as significant for communication as the meaning of the words. On the last day of our summer vacation, our family stopped in a cafeteria for breakfast prior to the journey home. We were in high spirits, anticipating our return after a great week together. But all this quickly changed as we entered the cafeteria. Because we were strangers we were slow in adjusting to the procedure. The man behind the counter shouted to us, "Get in line and give your order if you expect to eat!" We sobered up quickly. "Orange juice," I said. "We're out of it!" he snapped. "How about grapefruit juice?" I asked cautiously. In opening the can he cut his finger, letting out a volley of profanity that made me feel I was to blame. And so it went.

As we carried our trays to the table and sat down, we

felt deflated. Then I realized the man had failed to charge us for our beverages. I suggested to my son, who was especially downcast, that he return with me to the counter. As we again stood before him, the man barked, "Well, what now?" "I believe, sir," I said, "that you didn't charge us for the beverages." He thought a moment and said, "Yeah, that's right, I didn't." As I handed him the change, he smiled for the first time. "Thanks!" he said, "thanks a lot." We felt better after that—and I think he did too. Perhaps his immediate impression was that we were stupid to mention it, but at the subconscious level at least he may have felt a little better about his world.

As we have noted, listening is particularly difficult when one is threatened by what one hears. When we try to discuss political or religious views with persons who hold differing or even opposing views we can easily end up in an argument. Differences that are threatening tend to anger us. As the power struggle heats up, there is chaotic interrupting as everyone speaks—or shouts—at the same time in competing for the floor. When all the concentration is on speaking, there is obviously little listening. Our mouths are going so fast our ears cannot function.

If one is to be quick to listen and slow to speak one needs also to be slow to anger, "for the anger of man does not work the righteousness of God." Rather it is more likely to move us to abuse people verbally and otherwise. The prime example, again, is the abuse people heap on each other within the so-called intimate relationships. Most murders are "crimes of passion" within these relationships. The verbal attacks of mates, parents, children, and in-laws against each other destroy confidence and undermine self-respect. Anger leads to arrogance, and the tongue is the chief dispenser of this arrogance. Even swearing is considered a form of verbal arrogance. The humble person has no need to embellish with oaths his *yes* and *no*. There is no listening in anger, no empathy in arrogance.

As a reaction to a threatening situation anger is usually a secondary emotion. It is our defense against anxiety, hurt, pain, and guilt. Being slow to anger is not the same as *never* being angry. Some anger is legitimate—a justifiable human response to injustice. Even when it is simply a reaction to our own fears, it is still an indicator of those fears. For a guide to the expression of anger we look not to James but to an Old Testament psalm, quoted in the Letter to the Ephesians: "Be angry, but sin not" (Ps. 4:4; cf. Eph. 4:26). Not "Don't sin by becoming angry," or "Don't become angry," but *be* angry but not in a way that is destructive.

When anger is present it needs to be affirmed and not denied. Perhaps you have been in the presence of someone who is obviously angry but denies it? "Who's angry? I'm not angry!" Nor should anger be repressed, for then it slips out in indirect digs that are much more difficult to confront. *Be* angry when you *are* angry, but do not sin; that is, do not express your anger in ways that abuse others.

When Fred Hutchinson was manager of the Detroit Tigers baseball team, he devised a way of being angry that did not obstruct his relationship with the players.

Aware that he had a potentially abusive temper, Hutchinson would go to the locker room alone after a particularly exasperating game, lock the door, and then let his anger out on the furniture. When he had gotten it all out, he called in his players and was able to talk with them about the game without verbal put-downs.

Others let their anger out in prayer. The prayers may not be printable or even fitting in a church service, but they are nonetheless therapeutic. God can take our anger. His ego and self-esteem are not fragile like those of most people. After we affirm our anger in prayer, we are more able to confront the persons in question reasonably and with respect.

There are times also when we recognize the pattern of our anger and know from experience that ours is a distorted reaction based on old tapes we no longer wish to play. We acknowledge the anger and decide it is stupid. We dismiss it—cancel it—exorcise it—or otherwise turn it off. This is not repression, for repression is more unconscious than conscious, acting under the impulse of fear rather than the spirit of self-direction.

The I-Message

Anger is a natural, normal human emotion. In itself it is neither good nor bad; it simply *is*. What we do with it is the determining factor. The counsel to be slow to anger is based on the repeated awareness of how quickly and easily anger generates arrogance and all the destructiveness that stems from it. Despite this danger, anger has a potentially positive place in personal communication. This potential is based not only on the fact that it reveals what one is reacting against, but also on its own identity as a human emotion. The purpose of the tongue at such times is to reveal to those present where one *is* emotionally. This is what Parent Effectiveness Training calls giving an "I-message." The I-message follows the essential purpose of speech—to reveal oneself to another.

In contrast a "You-message" uses the tongue to "lay it on" somebody else. It is defensive rather than open. The I-message normally leads to understanding and intimacy, whereas the You-message stimulates defensiveness and leads to alienation. One who gives an I-message is taking the responsibility for his anger; with a You-message he is projecting this responsibility onto the other. The I-message is "I am becoming angry"—or "I am angry." The You-message is "You are making me angry." When a person transfers the responsibility for his anger to another, he is overlooking the fact that he is *permitting* the other to make him angry. Though it is comforting to think that one has no power to resist the stimuli of others, it is simply not true. Once someone accepts his responsibility even for his anger, he discovers the way to power that he previously had denied.

Using *I* rather than *you* as the pronoun by which to express anger communicates to others our own awareness of what is taking place within us. It is an expression of ourselves. Since the other is not put on the defensive as he is by a You-message, the way is open to "talk out" the feelings. Not only does such sharing usually dissipate the anger, but also those involved in the sharing know each other better as a result. Sharing at the feeling level strengthens the relationship. I-messages tend to break down the barriers that isolate us, creating a sense of belonging; they help us to know one another. The tongue is the instrument that assists others to perceive who we are—to penetrate beyond our physical appearance to our person.

IX

The Stains of the World

Let no one say when he is tempted, "I am tempted by God"; for God cannot be tempted with evil and he himself tempts no one; but each person is tempted when he is lured and enticed by his own desire. Then desire when it has conceived gives birth to sin; and sin when it is full-grown brings forth death.

Do not be deceived, my beloved brethren. (James 1:13-16)

My brethren, show no partiality as you hold the faith of our Lord Jesus Christ, the Lord of glory. For if a man with gold rings and in fine clothing comes into your assembly, and a poor man in shabby clothing also comes in, and you pay attention to the one who wears the fine clothing and say, "Have a seat here, please," while you say to the poor man, "Stand there," or, "Sit at my feet," have you not made distinctions among yourselves, and become judges with evil thoughts? Listen, my beloved brethren. Has not God chosen those who are poor in the world to be rich in faith and heirs of the kingdom which he has promised to those who love him? But you have dishonored the poor man. Is it not the rich who oppress you, is it not they who drag you into court? Is it not they who blaspheme the honorable name which was invoked over you? (James 2:1-7)

THE FIRE OF LITTLE JIM

If you have bitter jealousy and selfish ambition in your hearts, do not boast and be false to the truth. (James 3:14)

Where jealousy and selfish ambition exist, there will be disorder and every vile practice. (James 3:16)

What causes wars, and what causes fightings among you? Is it not your passions that are at war in your members? You desire and do not have; so you kill. And you covet and cannot obtain; so you fight and wage war. You do not have, because you do not ask. You ask and do not receive, because you ask wrongly, to spend it on your passions. (James 4:1-3)

Do not speak evil against one another, brethren. He that speaks evil against a brother or judges his brother, speaks evil against the law and judges the law. But if you judge the law, you are not a doer of the law but a judge. There is one lawgiver and judge, he who is able to save and to destroy. But who are you that you judge your neighbor?

Come now, you who say, "Today or tomorrow we will go into such and such a town and spend a year there and trade and get gain"; whereas you do not know about tomorrow. What is your life? For you are a mist that appears for a little time and then vanishes. Instead you ought to say, "If the Lord wills, we shall live and we shall do this or that." As it is, you boast in your arrogance. All such boasting is evil. Whoever knows what is right to do and fails to do it, for him it is a sin. (James 4:11-17)

Earlier we discussed the first half of James' definition of pure religion, namely, visiting the widows and orphans in their affliction. We now turn our attention to the latter half—"to keep oneself unstained by the world." The problem in this portion is identifying not only the stains but the world, and this has proved to be a most difficult task. Sensual pleasures have been the devil's decoy in misleading the church in this identification. Consequently "the world" has remained hidden and incognito behind the accepted institutions, structures, and attitudes of society.

The World in Our Culture

The world is contained in human society, with its cultural values, priorities, and norms. Culture is a human creation, with all the potentials for good and evil inherent in human nature. Yet it remains the creation of a fallen humanity. The failure to identify the world is the failure to perceive the basic fallenness of cultural values and priorities. Instead we frequently confuse these values with those of the Kingdom of God, buttressing this confusion with nationalistic and cultural religious sentiments.

In *The Pursuit of Loneliness* (Boston: Beacon Press, 1970), Philip Slater has provided a helpful critique of our culture in which he identifies its values and priorities in ways which clearly expose the world. The true character of a culture is manifested when choices have to be made between opposing values. The following are our choices as Slater sees them (p. 100), together with my own commentary on them:

Property Rights over Personal Rights. Even churches can be corrupted by this choice when they become property owners.

Technological Requirements over Human Needs. This choice has brought us to our present environmental crisis.

Competition over Cooperation. How many similar

organizations, from law enforcement agencies to churches, are undermining their efficiency because they are more concerned about credit than working together?

Violence over Sexuality. We are a violent people, with so little openness for affection and intimacy that we have to organize caring groups.

Concentration over Distribution. The imbalance created when a very small number of people control most of the earth's resources continues to feed Communist and racial revolutions.

The Producer over the Consumer. The power of big business and now also big labor has left the consumer with little representation.

Secrecy over Openness. This cultural choice was reflected in the Watergate imbroglio.

Social Forms over Personal Expression. Looking good is preferred to being good, even as manners are chosen over honesty.

Striving over Gratification. The destructiveness of worldly values is shown in this amazing choice in which enjoyment is rejected in favor of striving for it.

Oedipal Love over Communal Love. Using these terms Slater shows how the trend to invest our personal concern primarily into our immediate families makes family-centeredness as destructive to community as self-centeredness.

If there is any unifying principle in these choices, it would seem to be that we use whatever influence we possess in our own interests. Individuals and groups beyond our immediate family are seen as potentially either useful to these interests or threatening to them. This fosters a society of competitors who are so uptight about whether or not they are progressing that they cannot enjoy the life they have.

We might expect that such choices would bring a protest from those who perceive their ultimate folly. These are the prophets against whom the world reacts violently. Prophets demand radical change—at the roots—rather than surface rearrangement, and this brings on a life-and-death struggle with the world that accounts for the violence of its defense. "Which of the prophets did not your fathers persecute?" (Acts 7:52).

In but Not Of

How does one live in the world without being corrupted by the world? Being *in* the world and yet not *of* the world is a very difficult tension to maintain. Were it simply a matter of ethics or morals, the task would be easier. Instead it is a matter of values and priorities—of the orientation of our interests and the investment of our energies. People can be honest, decent, hard-working citizens and still be of the world, stained by its choices. This stain will be revealed when the press of decision no longer permits them to play games with others' values or to render lip service to values in which they have not invested. When we must choose between polarities, we make clear our identity—whose we are, God's or the world's. Assuming we are serious about preserving our identity, we need to sharpen our ability to identify the world.

Judging—Ultimate in Sin

The choices our culture is prone to make, as delineated by Slater, have the overall effect of pitting neighbor against neighbor. This coincides with James' position that the world is most clearly identifiable when it seduces us into becoming the judge of our neighbor. In "making distinctions among ourselves" we do the opposite of showing no partiality. Judging is the ultimate in sin because it is the ultimate in arrogance.

To judge another is to arrogate to oneself a position above the law. In fact, one is actually a judge of the law. This is obviously stepping outside the creaturely role and presuming to stand in the role of the Creator. Only God can exercise such judgment, being the lawgiver rather than being under the law. Therefore, it is the height of arrogance for a human being to presume to stand above another and judge him. "Who are you to judge your neighbor?"

When we presume to judge, we place ourselves in an illusional position of authority. The justification for this presumption is precisely the value system of the world, which is based on showing partiality. James cites as an example of this proneness to partiality the difference in the way even a Christian assembly may treat a poor man who comes into its midst with shabby clothing, and a rich man who comes in with gold rings and fine clothing. "Have a seat here, please," we say to the rich, but to the poor, "Stand there," or, "Sit at my feet."

The gold rings and fine clothing symbolize what is valued by our culture, while the shabby clothing symbolizes what is rejected. Both judgments are based on appearances rather than actual substance, and both are equally superficial. Those who adopt such values become equally superficial in their judgment of others, and the evil of their reasoning is clearly demonstrated in the discriminatory practices that blight our social order.

The irony in such superficial judgment is that those whom we in our culture elevate—those with the fine clothing and gold rings—are frequently our oppressors. Yet because of their cultural status they are able to appear respectable in their oppressions. The sins of the rich and powerful are made much less of in public opinion and before the courts of law than the sins of the poor and the powerless. Those on welfare who cheat, for example, seem to draw much more ire from the general populace than those who cheat in the upper echelons of business or government. The laws themselves are often written to protect the rich. For example, through legal maneuvering thirteen hundred Americans with incomes over $50,000 a year paid no federal income tax in 1971. Contrast this with the thousands who are accused of comparatively paltry offenses but, because they are poor, may spend weeks, even months, in abominable jails prior to their trial, because they cannot afford the price of bail. In the eyes of the world the poor are lazy. They could scarcely be more negatively labeled, in a value system based on striving and competition where "working hard" is the mark of a saint. "So let them go to work like I have to!"

When we are permitted by the world to pass this kind of judgment on our neighbors, we are also making it possible for others who qualify by the world's values to assume an air of sufficiency, power, and even righteousness that they do not really possess. Their arrogance leads them into an unrealistic sense of control over their own destinies. They assume that their exercise of power in the social order is power also over the future. James is under no such illusion: "Come now, you who say, 'Today or tomorrow we will go into such and such a town and spend a year there and trade and get gain.'" Come off it!

The Illusion of the Future

It is interesting that the example James gives of those who arrogantly assume that they can control their own destinies as well as those of others is the merchants. Even then the world was choosing the producer over the consumer. But those merchants were modest in their aspirations compared to the corporate giants of today who exert their control even over the destinies of nations and international relationships. When the Founding Fathers designed our republic, they were aware of the possibility of human corruption and thought they were protecting the nation against it by checks and balances of the three branches of government. What they did not foresee was the subsequent alliance of government with big business and big labor in the gargantuan lobbying enterprise with its spill-overs into campaign contributions and beholden office-holders. Instead of government monitoring these national and international enterprises, it is just as likely to be impotent before such pervasive power.

The big planners of the world—like the little planners—are obsessed with time. Like the farmer in Jesus' parable, when their plans are successful the only thing that comes to their minds is to expand their enterprise. The farmer chose concentration over distribution, and built bigger barns in which to store his surplus gain. Expansion, growth, progress are all values of a culture whose value system is focused on a gross national product. With so much invested in time, no wonder there is a need to control it—to assure the future. When so much of one's energy is invested in the world's values, it is difficult for one not to be *of* the world. The poor are prone to corruption also, but they do not have the vested interests to weight them in their choices. It is easier for them than for the affluent to be in the world but not of it.

Although those whose investment is in the value system of the world are future-oriented, they are not by that fact eternity-oriented. The cultural religion that goes along with these values often has a sentimental rhetoric about eternity, but the emphasis on the future is in time. This future orientation may cause one to miss out on values that are oriented to the present. It is in the present moment that eternity intersects with time. For this reason the two have been combined in the phrase "the eternal now." Those who strive for the satisfactions of the future are blocked by their own orientation from perceiving the eternal dimensions of life. In choosing striving over enjoyment they are failing to live in the present. Their goals are like the carrot in front of the ox that keeps him treading the mill. The macabre end of worldly values is symbolized in that carrot which is never reached. Fixed in an illusory future, it must remain out of reach to perpetuate the hoax. Yet those who have been seduced into treading the mill obviously believe that some day they will reach it.

Since the future is the focus for worldly values, those who adhere to these values need the illusion that they can control the future. Having chosen values that are disruptive to cooperation, they find trusting difficult. It inflates our ego to exert such control, even when it is illusory. Consequently, it is hard not to exploit what little control we have. At a pastors' conference where a particular plan for church financing was being presented, the question was raised how the congregations represented might respond to it. The pastor of one of the more prestigious churches replied, "How do I think St. Paul's Church will respond? I can answer that quite easily. I am St. Paul's." Ironically he lost his power in this church not long afterward. James would have had a quick word for him: "All such boasting in your arrogance is evil."

Actually we have no control over the future, even though we like to think we have. We cannot even guarantee that we will be alive in this future. "What is your life"—you who so confidently plan today or tomorrow to trade and get gain? "For you are a mist that appears for a little time and then vanishes." In the face of such transience, boasting of any control of the future is an arrogance toward life. The counterpart to such boasting is the massive denial of death which Ernest Becker believes characterizes our culture. We have chosen to forget the image of vulnerability that we saw in the mirror. We have repressed the awareness of our finitude. How fragile is human life! After the farmer in Jesus' parable had decided to build bigger barns to concentrate his gains, God said to him, "Fool! This night your soul is required of you" (Luke 12:20).

But even the fragility of human life is not predictable. At times we are equally impressed by the opposite—how tough, how enduring, is human life! Some who from a medical standpoint were not supposed to live, have lived.

Others who have fallen from heights considered beyond human survival have survived. So even what is probable may not happen. Therefore, those who "play it safe" with probabilities are still vulnerable.

What, then, is a more realistic approach to the future? "Instead you ought to say, 'If the Lord wills, . . . we shall do this or that.'" As a formula to repeat, this expression can easily be misused to serve the very purpose James is opposing. One can use the words "If the Lord wills" in reference to one's plans as a kind of magic protection, like knocking on wood. Those who use their religious piety to assist them in pursuing worldly values may use these words as a new formula for control—a ritual for pacifying the gods so they do not interfere with their plans.

For James the expression "If the Lord wills" is an acknowledgment of our creatureliness and of the eternal dimension to life. Saying the words can act as a conditioning exercise to achieve a perspective that is open to eternity. By the same token the expression can serve as a counteractive to the seduction of the world. "If the Lord wills" is a reminder of whose we are—that we do not own the future, and that our plans for this future are highly contingent. In the midst of time our times are in his hands.

Stain Begins with Desire

If one is stained by the world, how does it come about? We have been using the term *seduction*, following James' expression of being lured and enticed. However, James does not think of the world as enticing the individual; rather the individual is enticed by his own desires. As usual James is "dead" on excuses. One cannot blame God or the world when one succumbs to temptation—only oneself. The seduced is his own seducer!

Using language descriptive of the birth process, James gives a psychological analysis of the seduction process. Our desire when it has conceived gives birth to sin. The conception takes place when one is enticed—that is, when one embraces rather than dismisses the desire. When it matures, sin, which is the outcome of this conception, gives birth to—or produces—death.

Desire itself is a neutral term. Obviously, James is referring to a particular desire—desire for what the values of the world seem to promise. The progression of desire into sin is through desire's luring and enticing qualities. There might be no such progression if we were to face up to our desires—what it is we really want. Luring and enticing go with the games of double-mindedness. They depend on covert, hidden, and indirect dalliance. If we deal directly with our desires and with their satisfaction, there is no seduction game to confuse our awareness. When desire is out in the open, shorn of its seductiveness, we may decide we do not want to satisfy it.

The desire which conceives to bring forth sin and ultimately death is the coveting of power, possessions, and control. Its opposite is compassion. Without the lure and seductive trimmings, the invidiousness of this desire becomes apparent. It feeds on the cultural choices of concentration and competition, striving for the acquisition of pleasure in the illusional carrotlike future. The progression of such desire is ultimately death to the human spirit and to the human community. "For where jealousy and selfish ambition exist, there will be disorder and every vile practice."

The progression of desire into sin and death creates antagonisms between persons and between communities. The primal conflict it generates, however, is with ourselves. We have other desires and other passions which are directly opposed to it. The kind of person we become in our desire for the world is difficult to respect. One cannot be of the world and still be in harmony with one's humanity. What usually happens is that we project this conflict into our life with others.

"Whence come fightings and wars among you?" James is referring to community strife or feuds between communities rather than war as we understand it. Yet even wars between nations are still related to the conflict within the individual human being. Though we cannot focus our work for international peace on assisting individuals to come to peace with themselves, the tasks are still related. Nations and communities with internal conflicts, like individuals, need scapegoats upon which to project their frustrations. Because we do not, or cannot, integrate the opposing forces within, we desire but do not have. We lash out into our environment and discover we can integrate ourselves when the conflict is externalized. We attack and take what we could not receive. It is an old story. Yet for James such perpetual strife is neither justified nor inevitable. Instead he describes what could be realized in peaceful relationships if we had the wisdom to make value choices opposite to those of the world.

The human community unstained by the world, as James pictures it, is an attitudinal utopia in contrast to the dystopia created by those who are stained. He describes it as a "harvest of righteousness . . . sown in peace by those who make peace" (3:18). Peace is not simply the absence of strife, but the presence of qualities that draw us together—openness, mercy, gentleness, sincerity. Peace can be *made* even as war is made. As a culture we give rhetoric to peace, but we glorify our warriors, reflecting our double-mindedness and our attraction to violence. In contrast the Kingdom of God glorifies the peacemaker: "Blessed are the peacemakers, for they shall be called sons of God" (Matt. 5:9). *Blessed* is not a worldly appellation. Its reference is only to the present. The closest synonym is *happy*.

James does more than describe the unstained community in the abstract. Rather he gives a concrete description of its function. We turn to this functional approach to community in our final chapter.

X
Practicing Community

Every good endowment and every perfect gift is from above, coming down from the Father of lights with whom there is no variation or shadow due to change. Of his own will he brought us forth by the word of truth that we should be a kind of first fruits of his creatures. (James 1:17-18)

Therefore put away all filthiness and rank growth of wickedness and receive with meekness the implanted word, which is able to save your souls. (James 1:21)

Is any one among you suffering? Let him pray. Is any cheerful? Let him sing praise. Is any among you sick? Let him call for the elders of the church, and let them pray over him, anointing him with oil in the name of the Lord; and the prayer of faith will save the sick man, and the Lord will raise him up; and if he has committed sins, he will be forgiven. Therefore confess your sins to one another, and pray for one another, that you may be healed. The prayer of a righteous man has great power in its effects. Elijah was a man of like nature with ourselves and he prayed fervently that it might not rain, and for three years and six months it did not rain on the earth. Then he prayed again and the heaven gave rain, and the earth brought forth its fruit.
My brethren, if any one among you wanders from the truth

and some one brings him back, let him know that whoever brings back a sinner from the error of his way will save his soul from death and will cover a multitude of sins. (James 5:13-20)

We have seen what disrupts community; but what puts it together? In approaching this subject James uses a process analysis similar to that which he used with the origins of community breakdown. Community originates in God, the ultimate source of all light, who, unlike the sun as we perceive it, does not vary or cast a shadow. Everything good that we possess comes from him. He does not leave us to the enticement of our own desires. Rather he implants in us his Word of truth. This Word germinates and brings to birth in us the qualities of spirit that produce community.

Seeds of a New Humanity

Though the process is similar in development to that which brings forth sin and death, we ourselves initiated the process unto death, whereas God initiates the process unto life: "Of his own will he brought us forth by the word of truth that we should be a kind of first fruits of his creatures." The first fruits were the first of a crop to ripen, the implication being that the harvest is yet to come. The New Covenant in which the prophet Jeremiah had said God would write his Word on the human heart had replaced the Old Covenant of written tablets of stone. Those in whom this implanted Word germinates are the first of a new breed of humanity, making possible a new kind of community.

Though God wills on his own to implant in us his Word, we can count on James not to leave us without responsibility. While God takes the initiative, it is we who make a response to that initiative. The Word needs a response to germinate. *Response* and *responsibility* come from the same root word. Our responsibility, therefore, is to *receive* it.

The Word needs a receptive mind. A mind stained by the world is closed. It has to remain in control; it cannot trust. Anxiety keeps it hard at work, planning, worrying, keeping watch lest it lose control. So, says James, put away these worldly obstacles to receiving! Clear the mind, empty it, make it open!

This slowdown of the mind can be a cleansing experience. In its frenetic pace the mind tends to project its own fears and suspicions into its interactions in the present moment, and so does not receive the present moment as it is. In ceasing its defensive activity, the mind becomes open to the moment—can receive it. It can hear what in its corruption it could not. It is open now to the Word—to the God who speaks. The thoughts and feelings that continue to enter the mind to distract its attention from hearing can be shared instead in the openness of the moment, for in receiving the Word one is participating in the eternal dimension of life. When thoughts pass into prayers, isolation has passed into communion. The God who speaks is also the God who listens.

The Power of Prayer

For James, the creation of community has its foundation in a community of prayer. Desire when it has conceived and given birth turns us in upon ourselves. In fact, a traditional description of sin is *incurvatus in se*—the self curved in on itself. In contrast the Word when it is received turns us outward into community, the first instance of which is prayer. Whereas desire leads to isolation, the Word leads to dialogue—God's Spirit bearing witness with our spirit in inner dialogue—while community with others is the external dialogue. Though distinct, the two dialogues are not separable, for communion with God and communion with persons mutually support each other. Though the Word is implanted in the individual person, it is also uniquely given to a corporate body—what James and other New Testament writers call the assembly or the church.

We might not anticipate that a practical person devoted to action would also be devoted to prayer. Yet for James prayer is power *for* action: "The prayer of a righteous man has great power in its effects." As an example of such effects he turns once more to the Old Testament prophets, this time to Elijah in his conflict with King Ahab. As a judgment on the land of Israel for its idolatry, Elijah informed Ahab that there would be a long and severe drought. After three and a half years of it he informed the king that it was over. He then climbed on the top of Mount Carmel to await the rain.

As James tells the story, Elijah first prayed for the drought and then afterward prayed for the rain. The power of prayer rather than the ethics of Elijah's actions is the point at issue. The story is not told to glorify either the past or Elijah, but rather to provide an inspiration from the past for living in the present. Whatever legendary aura Elijah may have accumulated over the years is quickly dispersed: he was "a man of like nature with ourselves"—no more a giant than we in the present. If Elijah could experience the power of prayer, so can we. So do not be hesitant about recognizing and utilizing this power.

Prayer is not just a way of "laying it on God," but a way of opening ourselves to resources that he has already given us, both as individuals and as corporate fellowships. Healing is a case in point. The human body is equipped to resist disease and to fight it when it is present. These forces within us are at work for both the maintenance of and the restoration to health. Our spiritual and mental attitudes can affect these forces one way or another. When we pray for healing, it helps to keep in mind that we are also praying for the support of these resources already at work.

As part of my recuperation in bereavement I became a part-time hospital chaplain. In this capacity I prayed often with persons who were very ill, interceding for healing for them. I would also pray for the strengthening of their faith and hope and trust, "so that we might be open to receive that for which we pray." What is true of the body is true also of the total person. The implanted word is a force for growth and for health within our persons and within our fellowships. As the inner dialogue with God, prayer keeps us receptive to the Word already in our midst.

As the inner dialogue, prayer is an exercise in relationship, specifically in communication. Its power, however, does not lie in saying the right words; one is not using a formula to control the powers of divinity. Our involvement includes our total persons—our feelings, our imaginations, our faith. Elijah did not only pray, he prayed *fervently*. In other words, he put himself into it. Prayer is a concentration of our energies into the world of the Spirit. In interceding for others, for example, one identifies with them in empathy and imagination. Yet it is not empathy alone, but directed empathy. The milieu is not solitude but dialogue.

Though it is an inner dialogue, prayer moves us *from* ourselves. It is sharing with One who, though "closer than hands and feet," is still Another. The inner dialogue has the potential for a continuous sharing of our conscious awareness. James describes this continuum in terms of its polarities: "Is any one among you suffering? Let him pray. Is any cheerful? Let him sing praise." Joy as well as pain is the stuff of prayer. When James continues with his diatribe style, "Is any among you sick?" we might anticipate the same kind of response: "Let him pray for healing." But his understanding of prayer is not long confined to individual activity. God speaks also to and through the human community. Therefore, "let him call for the elders of the church, and let them pray over him."

The Healing Community

James describes the practice of community as a healing fellowship. The elders who pray with the sick are not simply older people, but rather are chosen by the community for their seasoned wisdom and spiritual leadership. In addition to praying over the sick person they anoint him with oil in the name of the Lord. The practice of anointing the sick had a long history even in

James' day. Originally it was thought to have medicinal value in itself. Later it became primarily a symbolic means for healing, as indicated by the accompanying words, "in the name of the Lord," and by its general use regardless of the nature of the illness.

God, as he is presented in the Bible, works through means. The sacraments of baptism and the Lord's Supper are rites which center in such means—*sacred* means. The water of baptism and the bread and wine of the Lord's Supper are means for receiving the assurance of God's presence and his love. The sacramental principle is operative beyond the sacraments as such to all of life. In the process of healing, the use of oil is a *symbolic* means for God's activity, while the use of medical procedures would be a *direct* means.

Symbols are important for the cohesiveness of community living. Community festivals center around such symbols, as do community traditions. The bread and wine of the kitchen table are more than food and drink to sustain life; they are symbols of fellowship. When symbols are sacramental in significance they are means by which the transcendent dimension to community life is realized. In the Lord's Supper, for example, the Communion being celebrated is with the members of the community and the presence of Christ simultaneously.

While the oil is a symbolic means through which God works, the "prayer of faith" is what will restore the sick to health. Even in prayer, faith is the energizer. In praying, one is reaching out in openness and receptivity. But there may be blocks in the way that need to be removed. Although it is the body that is ill, it may be necessary for healing to treat the soul also. If someone has committed sins, he will be forgiven: this is the gospel—the faith of our Lord Jesus Christ. But if the person is to realize this forgiveness—if it is to be a healing influence in his life—he needs to confess his sins. But again, confession is not simply an individual's talking out his guilt to God. Wisdom has shown that confession is best accomplished when carried out in the company of other persons. The fifth step of the Alcoholics Anonymous program is conducted with another person— usually one who is experienced in hearing fifth steps— because it is a confession. "Admit to God, to ourselves, and to another human being the exact nature of our wrongs." "Therefore confess your sins to one another, and pray for one another, that you may be healed."

By including the confession of sins to one another as an action of the healing community, James was following an old Hebrew tradition. It is also a very modern practice. Not only does total health care include the peace and health of the soul, but the sharing group in which confessions can be made is becoming more and more a part of professional therapy.

When people become ill—especially with a long and severe illness—they may wonder if they are being punished for something they have done. This is not the connection between sin and sickness to which James refers. The book of Job is a refutation of this notion, and James shows his knowledge of this in his reference to Job's steadfastness in his afflictions. Jesus too had discounted the connection when he answered in the negative the question whether a blind man was so afflicted because of his sin. This is not to say that sin has no effects. Besides being disruptive to community living, sin normally produces guilt, which alienates one in one's spirit. In their intricate interrelationship, spirit, body, and mind each affect the other, so that alienation of spirit can become harmful to one's total health. The antidote is forgiveness. This forgiveness needs to come from God as the One to whom we are ultimately responsible. But since we are in the realm of flesh and blood as well as in the realm of the spirit, we need also the tangible assurance of other persons. An accepting and sharing community has repeatedly demonstrated itself to be a healing influence for body, mind, and spirit.

The Caring Community

The healing fellowship is also the caring fellowship, where people care enough about each other to take the initiative in showing concern for the other. The illustration that James gives of such initiative—reaching out to someone who has wandered from the truth—is one of the most difficult to take. It is one thing to reach out to someone who you have reason to believe will be receptive and perhaps even appreciative, but it is another when you are concerned that your reaching out could be taken as a reproach. When a person "wanders from the truth," he is in a sense under judgment. Perhaps he has been seduced by worldly values or has become caught in the escapism of some form of addiction. Suppose someone cares enough about him to make the attempt to bring him back. To the wanderer it may appear that the person who takes this initiative is judging him. Actually his overture is the exact opposite of judging: it is caring. In a description of this overture similar to that of James, Paul emphasizes more the attitude behind it: "Brethren, if a man is overtaken in any trespass, you who are spiritual should restore him in a spirit of gentleness. Look to yourself, lest you too be tempted" (Gal. 6:1).

The caring person sees the wanderer as hurting, confused, and seeking to meet his needs in unsatisfactory ways. Unless he changes his course he may only be hurt more. This kind of concern assumes, of course, that the carer knows the way of truth. It is a dangerous assumption, hence the counsel to humility. Yet if one cares, it is an unavoidable assumption; hence the counsel to take the initiative.

Most of us are afraid that if we take such initiative, the other will take offense—will react emotionally—and we are uncertain about our ability to handle such feelings. It is much easier to "mind our own business." Normally it is good counsel in community living to mind our own business. Some of us have the tendency to want to control the lives of others; some of us tend to get our excitement vicariously from others' troubles. Yet when minding our own business means ceasing to care, the seeds for the destruction of community have been sown. One of the most lamentable signs of societal degeneration is the increasing number of incidents where people in desperate need have been ignored by others who did not want to "get involved."

Perhaps to overcome people's resistance to reaching out to the wandering, James "sweetens the pot." If as the result of making such an overture one is able to bring the wanderer back to the truth, "let him know that whoever brings back a sinner from the error of his way will save his soul from death and will cover a multitude of sins." Obviously it is worth the effort!

We cannot be absolutely sure who is supposed to receive these benefits—the one who is brought back or the one who brings him back. The one whose soul is saved from death is clearly the wanderer who has returned. But who is it that will have his sins covered? Actually it could apply to both. There is a similar expression in the First Letter of Peter: "Above all hold unfailing your love for one another, since love covers a multitude of sins" (I Pet. 4:8). To encourage people to make these overtures James may be saying that their efforts in caring will far overshadow the more negative aspects of their lives. A person may consider himself safe in minding his own business, but in accepting the risks of caring he is joining his life with those forces in society that build rather than destroy community.

The present is not predisposed by the past. Under the law of liberty there is the potential for change in every moment. When one who has wandered from the truth returns, he no longer carries the baggage from his past. He is freed from it by the advent of the new. Those who facilitated his return by risking themselves in the overtures of caring, are also beneficiaries. Not that their involvement will cancel out the judgment of a multitude of their sins. They are already forgiven. Rather the positive nature of their efforts covers—crowds out—the negative effects of their sins.

This description of community is for James the product of the implanted Word. The community is healing in its openness and acceptance, caring in its risking to reach out, and sacramental in its use of symbols and prayer. Actually this is a description of the church. James even defines it as the church when referring to the elders. The immediate context of his description for us, therefore, is not Alcoholics Anonymous or other therapy groups, but the church as we know it. The failure of the church to measure up to this model is one factor in the rise of these other therapy groups in our society.

There are people who for various reasons do not find it feasible to discover their community in their own congregation, although this would be the first logical place to investigate. Para-congregations can and have developed in neighborhoods or at work to meet this need. We profit from a supportive group in times of crisis. We also need such a group for the general maintenance of our total health. All of us need people in our lives who will aggressively reach out to us and at the same time be receptive and open; who can confront us gently in our faults and yet be accepting and caring; who can challenge us to actualize our potentials and yet comfort us in our hurts; who are physically affectionate and yet are sensitive in their spiritual awareness.

This description of the practice of community is a fitting close to the Letter of James and also to this development of its basic themes. The liberty that James affirms and the power that he sees as available through faith are appropriated not in isolation but in the milieu of interdependence with others. Our challenge within this interdependency is to invest ourselves into this potential for our development as persons—to affirm it, realize it, become energized by it—to do it now, do things differently now. We can also assist others to affirm their power for change and receive from others this same kind of assistance in our practice of community.